OXFORD MEDICAL PUBLICATIONS

SCHIZOPHRENIA

the**facts**

the**facts**
THE FACTS FROM OXFORD UNIVERSITY PRESS

ALSO FROM OXFORD
UNIVERSITY PRESS

SCHIZOPHRENIA

the**facts**

Second Edition

....

Ming T. Tsuang, M.D., Ph.D., D.Sc., FRCPsych
*Stanley Cobb Professor of Psychiatry, Harvard
Medical School and Director, Harvard Institute
of Psychiatric Epidemiology and Genetics,
Superintendent and Head
Harvard Department of Psychiatry
at the Massachusetts Mental Health Center
Boston, USA*

Stephen V. Faraone, Ph.D.
*Associate Professor of Psychology
Harvard Department of Psychiatry
at the Massachusetts Mental Health Center*

with the assistance of Peter D.C. Johnson

OXFORD
UNIVERSITY PRESS

OXFORD

UNIVERSITY PRESS

Great Clarendon Street, Oxford OX2 6DP

Oxford University Press is a department of the University of Oxford.
It furthers the University's objective of excellence in research, scholarship,
and education by publishing worldwide in

Oxford New York

Athens Auckland Bangkok Bogotá Buenos Aires Calcutta
Cape Town Chennai Dar es Salaam Delhi Florence Hong Kong Istanbul
Karachi Kuala Lumpur Madrid Melbourne Mexico City Mumbai
Nairobi Paris São Paulo Singapore Taipei Tokyo Toronto Warsaw

with associated companies in Berlin Ibadan

Published in the United States
by Oxford University Press Inc., New York

First published, 1997
Reprinted 1999

A catalogue record for this book is available from the British Library

Library of Congress Cataloging in Publication Data
(Data available)
ISBN 0 19 262760 0

Printed in Great Britain
on acid-free paper by
Biddles Ltd., Guildford and King's Lynn

Preface

The primary purpose of this book is to provide the intelligent lay reader with an introduction to the current state of scientific knowledge regarding the mental illness known as schizophrenia. Without in any way seeking to exclude the professional reader trained in psychiatry or any other branch of medicine, we are primarily concerned with helping the relatives and close friends of schizophrenics and those whose work may involve them in contact with schizophrenics, to understand the condition more clearly.

To accomplish this aim, we must of necessity employ some specialist terms from the vocabulary of psychiatry. In doing so, however, we have attempted to adhere to two guiding principles: such technical terms as are used will always be clearly defined, and we shall endeavour to steer clear of the use of jargon and psychiatric 'buzz words'—that is, the kind of semi-slang words that professionals in any field use among themselves as a convenient shorthand for more cumbersome terms with meanings that are mutually understood.

As we explain in the early part of the book, careless use of language has done a great deal to form false notions of schizophrenia among the general public. Equally seriously, the enthusiasm of some academics to generate new systems of classification, each with its new terms or, more confusingly still, new interpretations of existing ones, has served to make the study of schizophrenia more daunting to the interested layman and to create apparent conflicts of understanding where none in fact exist. Doubtless there will be those who occasionally find fault with our own choice of words; we hope they will at least concur with us that the quest for absolute linguistic unanimity is sadly, at present, chimerical.

Preface

Concerning references to research in the book, we have kept these to a minimum, partly for reasons of space and partly in order to avoid breaking into what we hope will be a relatively free-flowing presentation of the 'facts' promised to the reader. This is not an academic text and we do not feel it would assist the reader materially to know the source, date, and author of every study used in the book. Naturally, research projects of major importance to the study of schizophrenia are identified and documented more fully.

All names used in case examples, however brief, are fictional.

Boston   M.T.S.
January 1997   S.V.F.

the**facts**

CONTENTS

Contents

Section 1

What is schizophrenia?

Introduction

A case study

Twenty-six-year-old Janet Douglas (fictional name) was brought to a mental health centre in the United States. Upon admission she told the examining doctor she did not think she needed help. After further questions, she made the odd claim, with a straight face, that all the people in her city could hear what she was thinking. 'It all started five years ago', she said, 'when the President of the United States ordered the FBI to plant truth serum in my drinking water'. Suddenly, she broke into uncontrollable giggles, wrinkling up her face, rolling her head, and saying, almost incomprehensibly: 'But I fool them ... the way they are. My eyes can speak of the beauty. I say love-words and pattern words I've found out until everybody quits the way I make them ...'. She giggled wildly into her cupped hand. Shortly afterwards, she told the doctor that often when she 'starts to be perfect' she hears the voices of her neighbours in the air. They talk about her 'sins' and usually punish her by taking thoughts out of her mind, leaving her powerless to think. These voices frightened her so much when they came they deprived her of sleep and meals for as many as four days at a time. While she described her torments, however, her giggling faded and she became inappropriately calm, attaching no emotional depths to her own words, as if she were reciting a grocery list. Probed by her doctor for details about the strange voices, she fell silent; a crooked grin spread across her face with no apparent pleasure behind it, and thereafter she could respond only in single words to simple questions like 'What day is it today?'

According to her father's account, her symptoms had started when she was at college. Her childhood had been normal by anyone's definition, although she had few close friends. She went on to college where she majored in chemistry before dropping out. She worked at many jobs, but the lack of concentration which had begun while at college continued and the quality of her work deteriorated over a period of about a year. She took so many unexcused absences that she was dimissed three times before she finally stopped working altogether. At the same time, she lost interest in sewing, her favourite hobby, and ignored her former friends. She became irritable with members of her family, offering implausible and fragmentary reports of her activities and seeming to attach an incoherent private symbolism to the words and gestures of other people. The giggling, strange delusions, odd mannerisms, and broken manner of speaking had not begun until six months before her current admission to the hospital.

The diagnostic examination of this patient included a complete physical examination and laboratory report, which discovered no physical illness or injury, no definable physical disease process at work in her brain, and no history of drug abuse that could satisfactorily explain her symptoms or the earlier course of her illness. After all his observations, the examining doctor reached a diagnosis of schizophrenia.

Janet's case is typical of many young schizophrenics experiencing their first bout of the illness. As we shall see later in the book, her treatment and progress may take a variety of forms, but let us begin our exploration of schizophrenia by identifying some of the many widespread misconceptions concerning not only the condition itself but the very language used when it is discussed by professionals and laymen alike.

Defining the terms

What does 'schizophrenia' mean?

The term, *schizophrenia* comes from the Greek, *schizo* or 'splitting' and *phrenia*, meaning 'of the mind'. Hence, schizophrenia literally means suffering from a *split mind*. This portmanteau term, whose genesis we shall examine later, is perhaps one of the most unfortunate constructs in the English language. The great majority of technical terms from any science never find their way into everyday speech. 'Schizophrenia' and its variants, however, have become commonly used words, in the news media in particular, with infuriating results for those working to increase public understanding and sympathy for this harrowing and debilitating condition.

The term is normally misused in one of two ways. The first is due quite simply to a tendency to equate mind with personality; hence the schizophrenic is viewed as someone with two or more (for objects can split into any number of fragments) distinct personalities. Such a concept is perhaps inherently disturbing but its prevalence undoubtedly owes much to the popularity on both sides of the Atlantic of Robert Louis Stevenson's *Dr Jekyll and Mr Hyde*, a horror story of a man who deliberately cultivates by use of a potion a second personality possessed of great personal magnetism but a still greater capacity for rapacious evil. Although written in 1886, exactly 10 years before the first serious research into schizophrenia commenced, this book—quite bizarrely—served much of the twentieth-century public with their model of the typical schizophrenic. Deviating freely from the actual content of the book, they believed that sufferers of the condition were for the most part ordinary people who could uncontrollably turn into violent or even murderous villains. Sadly, this usage of the term can still be found in the seedier corners of the news media, and in particular the tabloid press.

In general, however, this crude view had, by the mid twentieth century given way to a less dramatic, but no less inaccurate interpretation. As science discovered more about the true nature of schizophrenia, the popular picture changed to portray schizophrenia as a more benign form of 'split personality', which renders the sufferer incapable of consistent thought or behaviour. At this time the term seems to have entered our common vocabulary as a metaphor for indecision, irrationality, or inconsistency. This form of misuse is still common today. A snippet from a glossy magazine provides the following observation by a popular actor: 'I'm truly schizophrenic concerning the arts; I really worked hard to develop my appreciation of ballet, but I don't have the slightest urge to acquire an understanding of the opera, which I know to be just as rewarding.' If only real schizophrenia was capable of producing no greater human misery than this!

There is a final sense in which the misuse of words has blighted the study of schizophrenia, and this is the tendency among clinicians and psychiatrists themselves to use variants of *schizophrenia* inconsistently or indiscriminately. In the past, any kind of 'nervous breakdown'— itself a vague and unhelpful term—might have been labelled 'schizophrenic' and the term was used by some as a kind of general label to describe patients suffering a wide range of types of derangement, depression, delusion, or personality disorder. Mercifully, this kind of linguistic abuse is extremely uncommon in developed countries today.

In conclusion, the reader would do well to adopt the guiding principle of forgetting any notions of schizophrenia picked up from the popular news media, or casual everyday speech. The correct use of the word *schizophrenia* is as a diagnostic term describing a specific mental condition that fulfils clearly specified criteria. The remainder of this book is concerned with presenting such information gathered by professional psychiatrists and researchers as would satisfy the average reader as 'fact', and in examining the means by which those suffering from the illness might be better understood and supported.

Historical background

Early research into schizophrenia

The illness we now recognize as schizophrenia was first described in 1896, in a study by the German psychiatrist, Dr Emil Kraepelin (1855–1926). The term he coined for the condition he observed was *dementia praecox*, literally *precocious* (i.e. unusually early) mental deterioration. Kraepelin's work was to serve as a basis for all future research into schizophrenia. His observations of patients suffering from dementia praecox formally identified for the first time many of the symptoms of schizophrenia and many of his diagnostic principles are still used by psychiatrists today. His work stands as a landmark achievement in the field of psychiatric research.

Kraepelin's work was to provide much of the base material and academic inspiration for the second great father of schizophrenia research, Dr Eugen Bleuler (1857–1939). It was Bleuler, a Swiss psychiatrist working at the beginning of this century, who coined the term *schizophrenia*, the linguistic source of which was explained earlier. As we saw then, this gift to the English language has in fact proved a mixed blessing!

As for the content of his research, it consisted in essence of extending Kraepelin's concept of the illness so that it included the main symptoms of **dementia praecox** together with those of **paraphrenia** a separate condition the latter had named to describe patients with delusions and hallucinations, but without other symptoms of dementia praecox. Bleuler listed the primary manifestations of schizophrenia as **thought disorder, emotional blunting** (that is to say an inability to experience normal emotions), and an impaired relationship with the external world. He considered thought disorder and emotional blunting, to be 'fundamental' or 'primary' symptoms of schizophrenia and *delusions* or *hallucinations* to be 'accessory' or 'secondary' to them. He examined his patients over a long period of time and concluded that, even after many years, patients always retained some significant residual symptoms. In other words, there was never complete recovery. We now know that this need not always be the case.

The work of these two early psychiatric pioneers is difficult to overvalue. Not only did it open the way for many other, primarily German psychiatrists, such as Kurt Schneider, Karl Kleist, and their followers, but it ensured that in educated circles at least the most extreme forms of *madness*, *lunacy*, *dementia*, *mania*, and a host of less restrained terms could be attributed not to demons or moral corruption, but to a disease of the mind.

The recognition of this disease may seem unimportant today, but it must be remembered that schizophrenia and its closely related conditions were then, as now, responsible for bizarre forms of mental delusion and behaviour. The classic 'madman' who waylays passers-by to impart a string of incomprehensible nonsense is in all likelihood a schizophrenic as are those sad figures at times seen clad in an eccentric collection of ill-fitting clothes, talking, laughing, or shouting curses at someone they alone can see or, more likely, hear. While identifying such people as victims of a named condition may have done little to alleviate their immediate plight, it certainly served to remove much of the morbid fascination they exercised on the public mind.

Have we then, nearly a century after Bleuler first used the word, reached a universally and unanimously accepted answer to the question 'What is schizophrenia?'. Reply to the question honestly, and the answer must be 'No'. This is not, however, to say that we have not reached the point where we possess standardized diagnostic criteria for clinical and research work. Moreover, the fact that not every psychiatrist in every country of the world adheres rigorously to them does not diminish their value. Indeed, too rigid an acceptance of any one particular definition might have counter-productive results were it to exist in the face of cultural and other variable factors.

International studies

The standard criteria we *do* possess began to evolve several decades ago when mental health clinicians and researchers realized that, without a standard description of schizophrenia, it would be very difficult to compare cases in one country with those in another or even those in one hospital with those in another in the same country. Clearly, any move towards standardization first required a study of the way that schizophrenia was *in fact* defined across international boundaries.

The first of these studies commenced in 1961, prompted by the observation by Dr Morton Kramer of the **United States National Institute of Mental Health** that a significantly higher proportion of patients were admitted to hospital for schizophrenia in the United States than in England and Wales.

A collaborative effort, called the *US–UK diagnostic project* set out to discover the reasons for this discrepancy. The project found that, when researchers used a standardized diagnostic concept and a structured interview form concurrently on two groups of 250 patients from New York and London, no substantial differences existed between the rates of schizophrenia in the two countries. The apparent differences in the rates of schizophrenia, were in fact due to the different diagnostic concepts of schizophrenia used by the hospital staff. In brief, the doctors from New York had a broader concept of schizophrenia than the doctors in London; many of the patients diagnosed as schizophrenic in New York would have been defined as manic-depressive by the doctors in London. Clearly, if substantial discrepancies were possible between countries and scientific communities as closely involved as those of London and New York, what of the world as a whole?

A more comprehensive study was launched by the **World Health Organization (WHO)**. The results of this *International Pilot Study of Schizophrenia (IPSS)* were reported in 1973 and in an updated form in 1979. The aim of the research was to discover the level of agreement or disagreement concerning the diagnosis of schizophrenia that existed between five widely differing geographic regions. In addition to the WHO headquarters in Geneva, local research centres were set up in nine other countries, five in developed countries, and the remaining four in developing ones. Using standardized information-gathering methods, statistical and computer analysis techniques, the researchers set out to discover the number of 'typical schizophrenics' in each centre, which features of the illness were most commonly present in the resulting sample, and which symptoms least likely to be reported.

The results of this research demonstrated widespread, if not complete international agreement concerning fundamental definitions of schizophrenia in psychiatry. It was clearly evident that the presence of hallucinations, delusions of being controlled by others, emotional blunting, and lack of insight were centrally important in diagnosing schizophrenia in all nine countries, while extreme mood changes were likely to be absent. This is not, however, to suggest that diagnostic criteria were shown to be absolutely standardized; when the original sample was examined it was discovered, for example, that the centre in the United States did not consider the presence of depressed or elated mood to exclude the diagnosis of schizophrenia; similarly at the Russian centre, diagnosis was based more on the course that the illness took over time than on the patient's symptoms.

The WHO study illustrates the current status of the diagnosis of schizophrenia in psychiatry. There is unanimous agreement among psychiatrists on the diagnosis of *narrowly defined typical schizophrenia*, but outside these limits there is some scope for disagreement.

3
Diagnosis

How do most schizophrenics come to be diagnosed?

Nicholas was 17 when he was brought by his mother to see the family doctor. Having enjoyed good physical health, he was not well known to the latter, but it seemed clear that the visit was facilitated by Nicholas's mother, who accompanied him to the door of the doctor's office. The mother requested a brief word with the doctor and explained that in the previous month her son, until then a perfectly normal boy, had lost interest in his usual diversions—sports and friends—ceased seeing a steady girlfriend and avoided family company at every possible opportunity. When asked if he had problems, his answers had been cryptic ('ask me again at two o'clock') or evasive. When the youth's father overheard from Nicholas's bedroom a 'surreal and disturbing one-sided conversation', he insisted that the general practitioner be consulted. The patient was clearly reluctant to talk; ordinary conversational gambits and specific questions regarding how he felt elicited no response. The patient acted distractedly shrugging or sighing when no question had been asked. On occasions he would mutter briefly to himself, his eyes fixed on an empty corner of the room or motion to the door in an obvious request to leave. After exhausting all normal avenues of communication with the patient, the general practitioner, suggested referral to a specialist (i.e. psychiatrist). This was met with further abstracted muttering, none of which the doctor was able to interpret or persuade Nicholas to repeat or clarify. The patient was referred to a psychiatric specialist for a full assessment.

It is to be noted that at this stage no diagnosis has been attempted or made. The general practitioner, presented with a young patient who appears to be psychiatrically disturbed and realizing that potential mental conditions are best evaluated, and if necessary, treated as quickly as possible, has referred Nicholas to a qualified psychiatrist for detailed evaluation. Indeed, very few initial visits to a clinician of any sort should be expected to yield an on the spot diagnosis.

The case we have just looked at shows just one of the many ways in which patients with psychological or psychiatric problems first come into contact with the medical service and are thence referred to specialists for diagnosis. Although in many situations the family general practitioner is in the psychiatric front line, and may be the first person to see the schizophrenic sufferer, families should remember that the diagnostic process may be relatively lengthy and involve a wide range of differently qualified clinicians.

We shall look later in the book at other ways by which patients first come to be diagnosed as suffering from schizophrenia, but let us first retrace our steps and take a more detailed look at the term *diagnosis*, which we have used until now in the commonly understood sense of 'determining what is wrong with a patient'.

What do psychiatrists mean by 'diagnosis'?

At its simplest, a diagnosis is a definition of an illness that has been agreed upon by most doctors. For psychiatric illnesses like schizophrenia, diagnoses are based on what scientists and clinicians have learned from their research and observations. They are not final definitions of well-understood phenomena, but rather working rules to help them to classify patients in a manner that will be most useful for their treatment and for scientific work.

Nonetheless, over time these rules and principles have been codified and set down to serve the psychiatric and medical communities.

Today there are several diagnoses of schizophrenia available. **The World Health Organization** maintains an **International Classification of Diseases** (*ICD*), which is currently in its tenth edition (*ICD-10*). ICD-10 includes rules for diagnosing schizophrenia and other mental disorders. This system tends to predominate in the United Kingdom, but it is by no means exclusively used for all cases or studies, and in practice there is always a degree of time-lag or overlap when psychiatrists switch from one edition to the next. At the time of writing, for example, the majority of practitioners in the United Kingdom are using ICD-9 in their daily work.

Another system was developed by the **American Psychiatric Association** and is included in the *Diagnostic and Statistical Manual* which is now in its fourth edition and known to doctors as *DSM-IV*. Like ICD-10, the DSM-IV definition of schizophrenia is set out in a series of clearly specified rules. If these rules are not satisfied, a patient should not be given the diagnosis.

For a psychiatrist to diagnose schizophrenia, five major criteria must be present from two major groupings: **core symptoms** and **course criteria**. If, however, any factor from the third major grouping, the **exclusion criteria** is present, a diagnosis of schizophrenia cannot be made. The patient's core symptoms may be present in abundance, and his course criteria fit the schizophrenic model to the letter, but if one exclusion factor is present, he will in all likelihood be diagnosed as suffering from one of the numerous complaints capable of mimicking schizophrenia with great accuracy.

The core symptoms criterion requires the presence of massive disruptions in thought, perception, emotions, and motor behaviour. These must occur for a significant portion of time during a one-month period (but this might be less if the patient is being successfully treated). These disruptions may take several forms. For example, patients might have bizarre beliefs (**delusions**) or they might frequently hear voices conversing with one another (**hallucinations**). Non-bizarre delusions are not sufficient to diagnose schizophrenia; neither are some types of hallucinations. To be diagnostic of schizophrenia, these must occur in the presence of one another or with marked disturbances of speech, motor activity, or emotional response.

The course criteria require that the time sequence of the symptoms and other aspects of behaviour follow a specific pattern. One of these requires that, over a period of time, the patient has shown a decreased ability to function effectively at work, in social relations, or in taking care of himself. Schizophrenia cannot be diagnosed if core symptoms are not associated with impaired functioning in the patient's daily life. Another criterion requires continuous signs of the illness to be present for at least six months.

The **exclusion criteria** indicate conditions under which the diagnosis of schizophrenia cannot be made, even if the core symptoms and course criteria are present. The patient must not have the marked disruptions of mood that would qualify for a mood disorder. Schizophrenia is also excluded if a known physical cause triggered and maintained the disturbance. For example, certain drugs can mimic schizophrenic symptoms. Schizophrenia-like symptoms can also be caused by neurological conditions such as epilepsy or brain tumours.

The clinician must be careful to eliminate any factors that might compromise a diagnosis of schizophrenia. Only when this has been achieved can the condition be said to have been *differentiated* from other conditions. Let us look now at some of the factors challenging a complete *differential diagnosis* of schizophrenia.

Differential diagnosis

Drugs and their misuse

I was so ... thunder-struck by what I actually saw, that I could not be aware of anything else. Garden furniture, lathes, shadow—these were no more than names and notions ... The event was this succession of azure furnace-doors separated by gulfs of unfathomable gentian. It was inexpressibly wonderful, wonderful to the point almost, of being terrifying. And suddenly I had an inkling of what it must feel like to be mad. Schizophrenia has its heavens as well as its hells and purgatories.

Aldous Huxley: *The doors of perception and heaven and hell*, 1954

Mescaline intoxication is indeed a true 'schizophrenia' if we use that word in its literal sense of 'split mind', for the characteristic effect of mescaline is a molecular fragmentation of the entire personality, exactly similar to that found in schizophrenic patients.

G.T. Stockings quoted in Robert S. De Ropp: *Drugs and the mind*, 1940

As we have said, it is possible for people to exhibit schizophrenia-like symptoms which are in fact produced by quite different causes. Several types of drug are capable of imitating aspects of schizophrenia, and it is worth examining this phenomenon in some detail.

The 'schizophrenia and drugs' topic breaks down into two distinct areas of study. The first is the use of so-called 'psychotomimetic drugs' by psychiatric researchers. Primitive experiments had been made in this field as early as 1919, but the bulk of this research was confined to the 1940s, 1950s, and early 1960s. Working with an arsenal of frighteningly potent psychedelics (the recently synthesized LSD and natural hallucinogens such as peyote, mescaline, and psylicybin) and 'super-amphetemines', a small minority of psychiatrists dosed volunteers—and often themselves—in the belief that the pseudo-schizophrenic state produced would assist their research into the illness. Many saw wonderful visions, while others descended into states of cowering terror. No one, however, returned from their trip with any useful insight into schizophrenia, since they had no experience of the illness with which to make comparisons.

This is not to suggest that these experiments were seen by all as a failure. Those psychiatrists who, like the layperson, Huxley, believed that one primary function of the brain is that of ordering perceptions in accordance with largely conditioned rules, thought that the disruption of this function by psychedelic drugs produces a state in fact very similar to schizophrenia. The logical way out of this impasse would be to give the drugs to a schizophrenic who had either recovered or was in remission and request a comparison. There are several problems with this proposal, however, not least the fact that the majority of these drugs are believed capable of triggering, if not actually causing schizophrenia in some people. Some psychiatrists, undeterred by this fact *did* 'treat' the illness with psychedelics during the 1950s and 1960s. This work—more 'pseudo-science' than science—did not show any therapeutic effects and provided no insights into the nature of schizophrenia. Today, such work would be considered unethical and dangerous to the welfare of patients.

The second aspect of the 'schizophrenia and drugs' topic is the use of so-called 'street drugs'. Considered as a social evil, this problem touches the lives of everyone living in the developed world today; for the medical and psychiatric professions, it presents a raft of other difficulties, among them that of muddying the waters of reliable diagnosis with regard to numerous mental illnesses, among them schizophrenia.

As noted above, the use of certain powerful psychedelics, such as LSD, especially over a lengthy period of time, can cause a range of symptoms resembling those produced by schizophrenia. Although frequently portrayed as a harmless recreational drug, the same may be true of cannabis, if used excessively. Stimulants, such as amphetamine and cocaine, are also capable of producing forms of psychosis. Long-term use of the latter is often associated with delusions of persecution (**paranoia**). Finally, MDMA or ecstasy, which at the time of writing is a widely used recreational drug, may well cause schizophrenia-like symptoms to develop in overdose or as a specific reaction in some individuals. Further research into both its short- and long-term effects is considered an urgent requirement by much of the medical profession.

Well-defined physical disorders of the brain and other organs

There are many well-defined physical disorders of the brain (i.e. diseases whose physical causes are clearly understood) which can cause some of the symptoms of schizophrenia. The most common of these are viral infection of the brain (**encephalitis**) and a particular form of epilepsy known as **temporal lobe epilepsy**. Obviously, patients with these disorders are not termed schizophrenic. Although many of their symptoms are indistinguishable from that of typical schizophrenia, there is usually some additional impairment of consciousness and memory. The patient's physical features (e.g. brain scan) or an examination of his cerebrospinal fluid will usually confirm that the symptoms are produced by a well-defined illness of the brain. Schizophrenia itself, which is believed to be a disease of the brain cannot be called 'well defined' since its causes and its physical manifestations in the brain are poorly understood.

Examples of well-defined brain conditions that may show schizophrenia-like features are: the early onset of behavioural changes due to reduction in the number of brain cells in old people; multiple areas of bleeding within the brain due to diseased brain vessels; syphilitic infection of the brain; Huntington's disease (chorea), brain injury, or brain tumour.

It is not only physical diseases of the brain that are capable of mimicking the symptoms of schizophrenia.

Physical illnesses, such as diabetes or malfunctions of the thyroid gland, liver, or kidney may also be culpable.

The last difficulty to be faced by the clinician in making a successful differential diagnosis is that of eliminating another group of conditions with no demonstrable physical cause, namely **mood** or **affective disorders**.

Mood disorders

Conditions affecting mood, like schizophrenia itself, may be brain diseases but their causes are poorly understood and any associated brain abnormalities difficult to identify. Like the well-defined physical diseases, they are capable of producing schizophrenia-like symptoms, but fortunately, the majority possess quite definite distinguishing features.

As we have mentioned already and shall discuss in detail shortly, a prominent symptom of schizophrenia is emotional blunting, a deadening of ordinary emotion. This factor alone helps psychiatrists to differentiate schizophrenia from manic-depression and similar or related conditions. A patient with this condition feels high (**mania**), talks continuously, brims with ideas, is cheerful, active or even restless, and unable to sleep, and may have delusions of being a religious leader or millionaire, for example. The manic phase does not, however, last and the succeeding low mood he experiences (**depression**) will be characterized by sadness, as well as slow thinking, movement, and speech. Loss of appetite and sleep disturbances are common, and the sufferer may feel that he is a great sinner who deserves punishment or even death. In extreme cases, he may attempt suicide.

Although manic-depression and other mood disorders may at times be extremely hard to distinguish from schizophrenia, their differentiating characteristics can be listed here quite succinctly. The thinking and behaviour of patients with mood disorders is governed primarily by the disturbance of their emotional feelings; the schizophrenic, in contrast, suffers emotional blunting. He may show behavioural signs of emotions, giggling, grimacing, and so forth, but these expressions are very often inappropriate and out of context.

Patients with mood disorders do not usually suffer from bizarre and implausible delusions. When they do, the delusion is consistent with their mood. For example, the manic patient might believe he is Jesus Christ and has returned to save the world. The depressed patient might believe she has caused the war in Bosnia and deserves to be punished. However, it is more usual for the manic patient to express plausible grandiose ideas ('I am the mayor of my village') and for the depressed patient to express simple beliefs of worthlessness.

A further distinguishing feature of mood disorders is the episodic course of mania and depression. A manic episode may be followed by a depressive episode (**bipolar manic-depression**) in succession with symptom-free intervals; or depressive episodes may occur alone (**unipolar depression**). In typical schizophrenia, however, complete recovery is usually rare, although the patient may have periods of remission with some residual symptoms.

Schizoaffective disorder

In saying that mood disorders and schizophrenia are usually readily differentiable, there are cases in which patients display both affective and schizophrenic symptoms, often in equal measure or in sufficient variety and intensity at different times to qualify for both conditions. These patients, who exhibit the massive disruptions of thought, perception, emotions, and motor behaviour characteristic of schizophrenia, together with severe aberrations of mood are termed **schizoaffective**.

Although the two classification systems we have mentioned, ICD-10 and DSM-IV give broadly similar definitions of this disorder, the exact relationship between mood disorders and schizophrenia is one of the 'hot potato' debates within psychiatric research. While the existence of schizoaffective disorder suggests to some researchers that schizophrenia and mood disorders may be the extreme ends of a continuum which covers all severe mental illness, the current thinking among most scientists and mental health clinicians is that these are distinct disorders. It is likely that some cases of schizoaffective disorder are variants of schizophrenia and others are variants of mood disorder. More research is needed to clarify the relationships between these illnesses.

4
Symptoms

We have now discussed schizophrenia in terms of the language used, correctly or incorrectly, to describe it; we have considered the work done by the psychiatric community to formulate practical working definitions of the illness and explained in broad terms the process and problems of arriving at clear diagnoses of schizophrenia.

It is now time to turn to the symptoms of the condition itself and to attempt by a combination of clinical data and real-life examples to show just what kind of psychiatric problems the schizophrenic may suffer. In view of the distressing nature of some of these symptoms we would like to assure families of men or women diagnosed as schizophrenic that their relatives are by no means bound to develop additional symptoms described in the following list. Schizophrenia can take many forms and it would be a rare patient who experienced all the symptoms presented in the following pages following their first bout of the illness.

There is a wide variety of specific signs and symptoms that will lead to the diagnosis of schizophrenia. These symptoms fall into two categories, **positive** and **negative symptoms**. Some psychiatrists characterize patients suffering primarily positive symptoms as experiencing the **acute syndrome** and those with mainly negative as exhibiting the **chronic syndrome**. More recently, some researchers have added other factors to what is basically the negative/positive contrast to formulate a diagnostic system based on two supposedly distinct forms of the illness, **Type 1** and **Type 2** schizophrenia. We mention this mainly to serve as an illustration of the sheer number of classification systems—we have ourselves mentioned several already and there are many more—the lay reader can confront in studying schizophrenia. All, however, recognize the distinction between positive and negative symptoms, whatever they may opt to call them.

Positive symptoms

These are the most obvious manifestations of schizophrenia. They are called **positive** because the disease has produced an abnormal event such as the creation of a sensation in the absence of something to be sensed in the environment or the generation of thought patterns that the patient cannot control.

Let us now examine these symptoms and listen to the experiences of schizophrenics and clinicians with regard to them.

Hallucinations

Janet, a 43-year-old schoolteacher had heard 'voices in her head' since her late twenties. In the early years these had been intermittent and had taken the form of 'a sort of echoed dialogue' with her own intentional thinking. She had not considered the matter serious and had not confided in her husband or doctor. In the past six months, however, the voices had become increasingly intrusive and quarrelsome, criticizing her appearance and behaviour and warning her that she would be 'punished' if she did not make efforts to improve. Her work suffered and she was encouraged to take six months sabbatical leave from her school. Eventually the voices were present constantly, threatening and urging her to harm herself in unspecified ways. Her husband now believed her to be having a nervous breakdown and it was at his insistence that she first visited a psychiatrist.

Auditory hallucinations Hearing voices, conversations, strange sounds, or even music—are among the most frequently experienced positive symptoms. The patient may hear one or more voices addressing him directly or any number of other voices commentating or criticizing his own thoughts or conduct. In some cases, these voices seem attached to distinct identities and the patient may even name them—'the joker', 'the critic', 'the schoolteacher', and so on.

Other forms of hallucination do exist and patients have complained of persistent and unpleasant smells (**olfactory**) or tastes (**gustatory**); of persistent pains (**somatic**) and of visual disturbances, such as repeatedly catching sight of a long dead relation, or being pursued by terrifying or disgusting animals (**visual hallucinations**). These types of hallucination are rare and are often discovered to be symptoms of non-schizophrenic mental disorders.

Delusions

The most common forms of schizophrenic delusion are those involving **thought insertion**, **thought withdrawal**, or **thought broadcasting**. As the names suggest, the patient suffering these delusions believes that thoughts are being inserted into his mind, causing confusion and disorientation; that they are being withdrawn, leaving his mind 'blank' or that a hostile outside force or device is causing his thoughts to be heard by others around him. Every general practitioner has his story of an otherwise normal and untroublesome elderly patient who one day confides, quite unconcernedly, for example, that the Russians have been using her as a sort of satellite to transmit messages' for as long as she can remember.

Thought insertion or **broadcasting symptoms** may be accompanied by quite bizarre beliefs. The man convinced that his boss wants to kill him may just possibly be correct; the man who believes his boss to be a robot—in all but the metaphorical sense!—cannot be right. Consider Paul's story:

A 28-year-old bank clerk, living in a large block of flats became convinced over a period of eighteen months that his private thoughts were in some way being broadcast to other tenants by means of a sophisticated network of 'thought detectors' concealed in the plug sockets of each room. He attributed this process to some sort of machine which was most likely hidden in the building's electic heating generator. He made repeated clandestine attempts to gain access to the room in which it was housed, which was naturally off-limits to all but the building's maintenance staff. Eventually, after several awkward late-night encounters with the building's janitor, he was found trying to break in with a crowbar. The police were called, and after questioning by officers and a police doctor, he was referred for psychiatric evaluation. After a full physical and psychiatric examination had been conducted in the ensuing week, Paul was diagnosed as schizophrenic.

We might mention, as an intriguing aside, that schizophrenic delusions tend to move with the times in term of their content. Paul's mysterious 'machine' is a case in point. As the modern world is driven increasingly by sophisticated communication technology, so the delusions of the mentally ill are increasingly likely to involve strange and sinister machines capable of affecting or controlling the individual in incredible ways. In what may be a related phenomenon, recently independent countries, which were once part of the British Empire, report a steady reduction in the number of schizophrenics who think themselves to be the Queen of England, around whom a considerable cult of personality was maintained during the imperial years.

Thought disorder and speech abnormalities in schizophrenia

Another class of positive symptoms is that affecting the patient's pattern of thought and speech. Aside from the problems they in themselves cause the sufferer, it is perhaps the quirks of schizophrenic speech that will most quickly alert the clinician to an underlying thought disorder at the point of diagnosis.

These thought disorders often take the form of *loosening of association*. As manifested in speech, the patient makes muddled and illogical conversation, often with almost surreal results. Relationships between ideas are disjointed or, to the listener at least, non-existent. Even stranger conversations may occur when the patient exhibits 'knight's move' thinking, where the patient constantly jumps ahead of himself, as if following his own, internal and quite bizarre set of connotations and associations. He may also 'talk past the point', producing rambling and complex responses to even simple yes/no questions. At its most pronounced, loosening of association may show itself as 'word salad' or verbigeration, an incomprehensible jumble of words which despite on occasions containing almost poetic imagery and associations, is totally incomprehensible to the listener.

Negative symptoms

Positive symptoms are in some ways the most dramatic aspects of schizophenia, and they are certainly likely to be the most rapidly and harrowingly visible to relatives of the sufferer. This is not, however, to suggest that the so-called 'negative symptoms' are not in their own way equally serious for the patient. Negative symptoms, are those which feature the reduction or even obliteration of normal mental or behavioural processes. As such, they may be every bit as debilitating and disturbing for the patient and those close to him as those in the former category.

There are, not surprisingly, several different ways of classifying negative symptoms. Among the simplest and most helpful is the system devised by Dr. Nancy Andreason of the University of Iowa, and it is her classification we shall set out here. Dr. Andreason identifies five distinct groups of negative symptoms.

Affective flattening or *emotional blunting* refers to impairments in the ability to express emotion by both verbal and non-verbal means. Normally, people convey their emotions by means of a complex system of language and gesture, fitting appropriate bodily movements to the messages they are conveying so as to reinforce or emphasize them. Among such gestures are facial expressions such as frowns or smiles, hand movements, bodily posture, tone and volume of speech, and so on. The schizophrenic patient, in contrast, does not convey emotion in this manner. This is not a matter of choice; he simply does not have the expressive capacity of the ordinary individual. Indeed, in some cases, he does not even experience the internal sensation of emotion.

The second grouping is named **alogia**, and relates to the speech characteristics noted in schizophrenic patients. One common symptom within this group is known as **poverty of speech**, meaning simply that the patient says little and rarely initiates conversation. In other cases, the patient may talk but his speech, although not bizarre, conveys little meaning. This symptom is termed **poverty of content of speech**. Some patients produce speech that is meaningful but they periodically stop speaking and restart after an interval of time. This is termed blocking. Consider this excerpt from a casual conversation with Nick, a 26-year-old man diagnosed as schizophrenic four years earlier:

Psychiatrist: How are you today, Nick?
Nick: (silence)
P: Did you enjoy your breakfast?
N: (after a long pause) I didn't understand …
P: Your breakfast. Do you remember, you weren't enjoying your food?
N: (silence)
P: What did they give you for breakfast today?
N: Please would you ask me again … (long pause of three minutes) … I really can't answer that now.

Speech patterns of this type are highly characteristic of schizophrenics experiencing thought-blocking. In extreme cases, the pauses could, if permitted to run their course, last for literally hours. Their speech may otherwise appear normal, but their long delays in responding can be irritating to others.

Avolition, the third category, describes a state in which patients seem almost to lack the *volition* or *will* to act at all. They may respond to stimuli provided by others but if unprompted they may not speak, move, or engage in any other activity. The term 'apathy' is used in a technical sense to describe this symptom, and indeed the patient conforms to our notion of everyday apathy, albeit in such an extreme form that the individual seems listless and unmotivated to the point of total unconcern for the world around him.

Naturally, we cannot see and examine a patient's will—even if such a thing exists as an independent entity—so the clinician must infer the patient's level of motivation from observable signs. The signs may be quite subtle: a lack of persistence at work or school and a tendency to sit and do nothing for long periods can have many causes, particularly during adolescence. Other signs, however, are far more simple to detect. One of these, lack of self-care, may be taken to extraordinary limits by acutely ill schizophrenics, taking almost grotesque forms. An account of one schizophrenic's appearance from a medical case study gives an indication of this:

> When presented for examination, the patient, a 32-year-old man was bizarrely attired and visibly unclean. His shoulder-length hair was dirty and matted and his face almost hidden by a wild growth of beard. His clothing was dirty and quite inappropriate to the warm weather outside. Over several layers of ragged shirts and sweaters he wore a large ex-army trenchcoat, belted with a bent coat-hanger and decorated with an assortment of stickers, badges, and small objects attached with string. A filthy baseball cap perched undone on his head and a pair of training shoes covered with plastic carrier bags completed his garb.

If the description calls to mind many 'down-and-outs' roaming the streets, one should not be surprised; as we shall have cause to consider later in the book, a high proportion of these sad characters are indeed schizophrenics.

Dr Andreason's fourth grouping of negative symptoms is primarily characterized by **anhedonia** (the inability to experience pleasure to a normal degree) and **asociality** (avoidance of the company of others). In the schizophrenic these tendencies may be so pronounced as to leave little doubt of the illness's influence. The patient may have no recreational interests whatsoever. The asocial patient may have no friends or acquaintances at all, but not regard this as a problem. At the same time, he will also have no romantic or sexual interests due to a decreased ability to feel intimacy with others.

Finally, the most extreme form of negative symptoms are seen in **catatonia**. These include **negativism, mutism, waxy flexibility, posturing,** and **catatonic stupor.** **Negativism** refers to the refusal to comply with the most reasonable requests for no discernible reason. **Mutism,** as the word suggests, occurs when a patient completely refuses to speak. Although it is uncommon, some patients may enter a **catatonic stupor.** While in this trance-like state they may exhibit **waxy flexibility,** a condition sometimes called **catalepsy.** In this state the patient, having been advised that he is not expected to co-operate, and if necessary, being distracted by conversation, can be posed by the doctor like a marionette. The patient will then hold this pose for at least several minutes, even if the position appears uncomfortable. **Posturing** occurs when the patient himself adopts an unusual, and at times strangely contorted position for a considerable time.

Subtypes of schizophrenia

In describing the symptoms of schizophrenia we have mentioned several terms which the lay reader may have seen coupled with the word, **schizophrenia.** Examples would be *paranoid*: one often hears sufferers described in the media as 'paranoid schizophrenics', meaning someone who believes himself to be the object of persecutional plots by others. Another commonly mentioned type is **catatonic schizophrenia**, which renders the patient withdrawn to the point of a virtual 'waking coma'. Less often heard mentioned in lay circles is **hebephrenic schizophrenia**, a condition in which the patient's emotions are disturbed and confused to the point where, for example, news of the death of a close relation is met with howls of laughter or amused indifference.

These subtypes are included in the diagnostic systems ICD-10 and DSM-IV as **schizophrenia** or **schizophrenia-like disorders** (together with several others, such as **undifferentiated** and **residual schizophrenia**), and are used by clinicians in their diagnoses. Hence, a patient's condition might be described as *schizophrenic*, *paranoid*, or *chronic*.

Although this method of classification is almost universally used, it should be pointed out that there are psychiatrists who believe this sort of categorization unhelpful. For example, no support was found for its use in the WHO *International Pilot Study of Schizophrenia (IPSS)*, and some clinicians feel that it 'brands' a sufferer as a certain sort of schizophrenic when, at another diagnostic session, he or she might exhibit quite different dominant symptoms. The authors feel that while this argument carries some weight, the need for a standard system of classification overrides such concerns.

We shall look at some of the other major subtypes of schizophrenia later in the book.

Section 2

Schizophrenia: the central questions

Introduction

Knowledge is two-fold, and consists not only in an affirmation of what is true, but in the negation of that which is false.

Charles Caleb Colton: *Lacon*. 1825

Facts is stubborn things.

Attributed to Henry Ford

In the previous section of this book, we described the main symptoms of schizophrenia and the means by which it is diagnosed. In addition, we attempted to clarify at least some of the confusion and misconceptions associated with the illness, and to identify the scientific research that has most helped to shape our understanding of it.

Having set out the basic facts of what schizophrenia *is*, we can now turn to the questions to which any researcher, or indeed any interested lay person would naturally seek answers. Some of these questions routinely form the basis of research into any medical complaint, while others are particular to the study of schizophrenia; all, however, must be considered, if not answered, as part of any serious enquiry into the condition.

The fact that these 'central questions' concerning schizophrenia are posed only after describing the state of current knowledge of the illness is, of course, a convenient artifice employed to make this book easier to read and understand. In the 'real world' researchers do not await full and conclusive evidence regarding the basic nature of an illness before proceeding to more advanced forms of enquiry. Kraepelin and Bleuler, for example, may have known little of genetics (Gregor Mendel's first experiments into heredity had only begun in 1865), but this could not have prevented them from wondering how schizophrenia was developed or transmitted. In fact, many of the questions we shall examine have been researched repeatedly since the first identification of schizophrenia, long before the discovery of the particular scientific method which alone could help to answer them. In view of the inconclusive nature of our current understanding of many aspects of the illness, this may still be the case today.

What are the central questions of schizophrenia?

There are many ways of examining the topics covered in the forthcoming chapters and the device of framing them as questions may not appeal to all tastes. Similarly, the questions themselves could be posed in many different ways. We have, however, chosen to ask:

(1) How common is schizophrenia?

(2) Is it caused by hereditary or environmental factors?

(3) What sort of disease is it? Specifically, is it a disease of the brain?

(4) Can it be prevented, alleviated, or cured?

In the following chapters we shall assess the progress made by psychiatric researchers into the first three questions. The last question, which is likely to be of greatest interest to those with schizophrenic relatives, will in effect act as a starting point for the material in the remaining sections of the book.

6 How common is schizophrenia?

Some questions of methodology

We have already seen in our discussion of the *US–UK Diagnostic Project* that the number of schizophrenic people in a given population will vary according to the diagnostic definition of schizophrenia adopted by those researching the question. This being the case, the most accurate evaluation of the question, 'How common is schizophrenia?' ought in theory to be achieved by limiting one's research data to an area (e.g. the United States) in which one and only one definition is used (DSM-IV, perhaps). This, however, raises two problems, the first theoretical and the second practical. If data are drawn from one country alone, the danger exists that the results will be culture-specific; conduct your study on another continent and you might achieve quite different results. There is also a practical objection to limiting data in this way, namely that if one is to consider (as one doubtless ought) the best and most reliable research, one will find that it has actually been conducted in a number of different countries and using a heterogeneous range of methodologies.

We shall, therefore, draw on scientific research conducted in different countries. This may, in fact, have the effect of reducing, if not eliminating cultural bias, although it would be incorrect to make such an assertion in our current state of knowledge. We shall, in any case, return to the question of cultural influences on schizophrenia and its study at a later stage in the book.

Terminology

What exactly is meant by the word 'common', in psychi-atric research? In literal everyday speech the word may, according to context, mean: how much or how many of something exists; how often it is encountered, or what one's chances are of meeting with it. For the purposes of research into schizophrenia, three factors are considered. These are: the **prevalence rate**, achieved by dividing the number of cases of the disorder by the total number of a given population; the **incidence rate**, that is the number of new cases to appear within that population over a given period; and the **lifetime risk**, or probability that a person will acquire the illness at particular phases of his or her life. No single calculation of these factors will provide an exact answer to our question; they must rather be consid-ered together if possible with reference to one clearly delineated sample group.

Prevalence rate

The prevalence rate of schizophrenia is customarily reported as the number of cases per 1000 people surveyed within a one-year period (a one-year prevalence per 1000). Various international studies have found rates varying from a low of 0.6 per 1000 to a high of 17 per 1000. This high rate of discrepancy may be due to the sim-ple fact that in any study one has no guarantee, no matter how large one's sample, that it will be truly representative of the population as a whole; more likely, however, the disparity is the result of the studies having taken place in different countries, with differing methodologies, diagnos-tic criteria, and sample sizes. This variability does not, however, follow any simple or consistent pattern with regard to the country in which the study was conducted. Whether we consider East versus West or developed ver-sus undeveloped countries, most studies find between 3 and 10 per 1000. The international prevalence rate of schizophrenia is agreed to be approximately 0.5 per cent.

In the 1980s, the United States National Institute of Mental Health launched the *Epidemiological Catchment Area* (ECA) study of mental illness in several American cities. The prevalence rate of schizophrenia was 6 per 1000 in St. Louis, 11 per 1000 in New Haven, and 10 per 1000 in Baltimore. By way of comparison, a 1994 study conducted in the United Kingdom, the OPCS *Survey of Psychiatric Morbidity* produced a figure of approximately 4 cases per 1000 for people aged between 16 and 64.

Incidence rate

As we can see, the variations achieved in prevalence rate studies suggest that it cannot alone proffer a wholly credible response to our question. If we are to discover how commonly schizophrenia occurs we must also consider other statistics. The incidence rate differs from the prevalence rate in that it considers only the incidence—or first occurrence—of schizophrenia cases. To compute an incidence rate, we must possess a definition of when schizophrenia first begins and this, given the subtlety of certain symptoms and the difficulty of pinpointing an exact time for when a pattern of behaviour becomes sufficiently exaggerated or troublesome to betoken mental illness, is no easy matter. For this reason, incidence rates are usually calculated by reference to a patient's first visit to psychiatric services while suffering schizophrenic symptoms.

The incidence rate is usually expressed as the number of new cases in a given period per 100 000 population; past studies have indicated an average rate of 21.8 per 100 000 per year. As we have stressed earlier, these figures cannot be taken entirely at face value owing to the different methods used to obtain them. Like the prevalence rate, however, they do not seem to differ greatly according to time or geographical area.

Lifetime risk

Studies of schizophrenia show that most patients tend first to fall ill between the ages of 20 and 39 years of age. This is known as the **risk period** for schizophrenia. Importantly, men tend to succumb to the illness significantly earlier than women. One side-effect of this fact is that any study of the incidence rate of schizophrenia will necessarily be affected by the sex and age distribution of the sample chosen.

The age distribution of sufferers is particularly important when estimating the likelihood of a person becoming schizophrenic within his lifetime, that is his **lifetime risk** of contracting the illness. When calculating lifetime risk, researchers consider all persons younger than 20 as not having reached the risk period and all those older than 39 as having passed it. The number of people studied can then be adjusted according to the age distribution of the population. Lifetime risk is then estimated by taking the number of schizophrenics in a population as a numerator and the age-adjusted number of people exposed to the risk as a denominator. The reported figures from various studies—including the American survey of cities cited earlier—tends to yield results ranging from 0.3 per cent to 3.7 per cent. When many studies are taken together, the lifetime risk for schizophrenia in the general population emerges as approximately 1 per cent.

Great caution should be exercised in ascribing too much credence to the precision of these figures. Considered beside the general population, schizophrenics suffer a higher death-rate, many may be in remission at the time of the study, while others may 'slip through the net' in a variety of ways. These factors considered, the lifetime risk rates for the illness are far more variable than the prevalence or incidence rates.

The differences in magnitude of the prevalence, incidence, and lifetime risk rates emphasize the importance of using these terms correctly. As our discussion shows, the risk of developing schizophrenia over one's lifetime is

7
Is schizophrenia inherited?

A case study

Timothy Lamb was 22 when he first appeared at his general practitioner's office, accompanied by his girlfriend who explained that he was 'hearing voices' and apparently suffering from delusions. As a newly registered patient, he was not well known to the doctor, and it became clear during the initial formalities of the consultation that he was there largely at the behest of his girlfriend who was deeply worried about him. The patient himself was extremely reluctant to answer questions about himself and his girlfriend provided the background to his visit. He had always, she explained, been 'eccentric', even 'kind of crazy', talking in a strangely rhythmic manner, rich in bizarre imagery, puns, and quickly constructed epigrams. She recognized that this was far from normal but conceded that she found it somehow appealing. He lived alone; she had never met his parents and he never mentioned them save in rare nonsensical asides. Although their relationship was 'wonderful', she had recently become concerned by his behaviour. He would remain silent and withdrawn for long periods of time, unless firmly prodded into activity and, more worrying still, he would often speak when not addressed, as if responding to voices only he could hear. The 'final straw' came when, at her prompting, he emerged from one such bout of torpor in a confused and angry state and lashed out at her. He was instantly apologetic, claiming that he had mistaken her for his father 'with whom he had been arguing'. At her insistence he agreed to accompany her to the doctor. His general practitioner referred him to a psychiatric unit where the consultant diagnosed schizophrenia.

In the course of Timothy's subsequent treatment it emerged that his family life had been unusual, in that his parents had divorced soon after his birth and he had been brought up entirely by his mother, who was generally considered 'eccentric' or even 'odd' by most who knew her. She dressed eccentrically, wearing brightly coloured clothes in wildly clashing combinations and her appearance was generally Bohemian. Her views on parenting were extremely non-conformist, stemming from the central opinion that children possessed superior 'natural instincts' to adults, and should therefore be left as much as possible to make their own decisions about everyday matters. Timothy had been allowed almost total freedom while growing up, deciding his own bedtime and choosing his own diet, clothes, and activities. There had been several clashes with the educational authorities over his frequent absences from school but he was generally happy if somewhat detached at school and his attendance record was sufficiently good for him to avoid expulsion.

Asked about any known history of mental illness in the family, his mother reluctantly admitted that she had undergone treatment for extreme postnatal depression which led her to 'go completely insane' for a while. She also seemed to remember that her grandfather was always described as being in some way 'strange'. Asked if she considered Timothy himself to be suffering from a mental illness, she said that she personally doubted it; she had not known that he was hearing voices, but admitted that she would not in any case have seen that alone as particularly important. 'We all hear voices sometimes', she said, 'the important thing is what they say to us.'

There is nothing new about the idea that mental illness, like other types of disease can 'run in families', but it is no simple task to transform this simple piece of folk wisdom into a verifiable scientific proposition. Several problems immediately spring to mind. When the research involves considering past generations, there is likely to be a shortage of well-documented clinical data reporting their condition. There is also the difficulty of deciding just what degree of 'eccentricity'—for this kinder term is frequently used of the deceased—can be assumed to be a euphemism for real mental illness. Such problems cannot be conclusively solved or eradicated. Scientific method involves the same measure of 'common sense reasoning' as any other field of enquiry; the researcher must at times do the best with what he has and hope that the results he obtains will be given credence—and eventually unanimous acceptance—by being repeated when others conduct similar empirical research.

These practical difficulties aside, the challenge facing the researcher concerned with identifying the 'cause' of schizophrenia is twofold. First, he or she must investigate the possibility of genetic transmission, and second, assess the role of environmental factors in producing or modifying schizophrenic symptoms.

Does schizophrenia run in families?

Studies into this issue were first undertaken in Europe over half a century ago. Broadly speaking, their conclusions were affirmative: parents, brothers, and sisters of sufferers were on average 10 times more likely to develop the condition themselves than members of the general population; for children of schizophrenics, the risk was still higher, approaching 15 times. More distant relations, while still suffering a greater than normal chance of becoming schizophrenic, were at considerably less risk than members of the immediate family circle.

Contemporary studies using more rigorous research methods and narrower, more precise definitions of schizophrenia have also found the illness to run in families, but the risk figures reported have tended to be lower. For example, one large family study, conducted in Iowa by the principal author of this book and his colleagues, reported a risk to brothers and sisters of contracting the illness as approximately 3 per cent. Although this is far lower than the figure yielded by the early European studies, it is still some five times greater than the risk to relations of non-schizophrenics.

Although these family patterns strongly suggest a hereditary basis for schizophrenia, they could also be explained by reference to shared environment. Clearly, some means is required to disentangle these two factors if family studies are to retain their validity. The simplest and most reliable means of achieving this is to study twins and adopted children.

Twin and adoption studies have played vital parts in research into schizophrenia and we shall consider both in some detail. This will, of necessity, entail the presentation of some relatively complex statistical and scientific data, but we have attempted to present these as transparently as possible. If you find the 'heavier' passages too difficult to take in easily, please at least search out and note the *conclusions* or key points of the research in question. (If even these seem unclear, the fault probably lies with the authors!)

Heredity and responsibility: a brief digression

When considering the transmission of any illness from parent to child, a certain degree of sensitivity is required. Some parents on discovering that an illness may have been passed to their child through their genes can feel a degree of responsibility or even guilt. These feelings may persist even in the face of clear scientific or statistical evidence that they took no unreasonable risk in conceiving the child. This is particularly the case with exceptionally harrowing illnesses like schizophrenia, whereby parents may see their children's mental health deteriorate to the point where they are virtually unrecognizable as their former, healthy selves.

If you are reading this book as the parent of a schizophrenic person, we hope that you will not be disturbed by the misconception—for a misconception it surely is—that you are in some way to blame for your son or daughter's illness. It is true, as we shall discuss later in the book, that the family can, by its collective behaviour, serve to worsen the sufferer's symptoms; but more importantly, its members can do a great deal to alleviate the condition of the illness and to assist the sufferer. This book does not purport to be a help manual for those close to schizophrenics, but we feel that the very fact that you have chosen to read it implies that you are searching for a greater understanding of how best to support those with the illness. Misplaced self-blame, apart from making you feel bad in itself, will only render you less able to provide that support.

Twin studies

There are two types of twins: identical and fraternal. Identical twins come from one fertilized egg and therefore have identical sets of genes. Fraternal twins come from two different fertilized eggs and hence share only half their genes; they resemble ordinary brothers and sisters but shared the same uterine environment before birth.

If both twins of a pair are schizophrenic, we say that they are **concordant** for schizophrenia; if only one is schizophrenic, they are described as **discordant**. The percentage of concordant pairs out of a total number of pairs of twins in which one is schizophrenic is known as the **concordance rate**.

Clearly, if schizophrenia were due entirely to genetic factors, the concordance rates for identical and fraternal twin pairs would be 100 per cent and 50 per cent, respectively, the same percentage as governs the sharing of their genetic make-up as a whole. If the concordance rate for schizophrenia among identical twins was significantly higher than that of fraternal twins—although less than 100 per cent—this would suggest a strong genetic component in schizophrenia. If, finally, there was found to be no difference in concordance rates between identical and fraternal twins, genetics would appear to play no discernible role in schizophrenia, and we would have to look to entirely environmental factors to explain the familial transmission of the illness, since shared environment would be the most obvious factor uniting the twins.

The potential value of twin studies should be obvious from these propositions, and such studies have indeed been undertaken by many researchers all over the world. If we pool their results, we discover concordance rates of approximately 53 per cent for identical twin pairs and 15 per cent for fraternal twins. This can be taken as evidence of the presence of a hereditary component in schizophrenia, but the fact that the concordance rate for identical twins falls far below 100 per cent indicates that other causal factors are involved in the production of the illness.

It must be noted that not every researcher is entirely satisfied with the value of these studies. It has been argued, for example, that being raised as a twin can confuse self-identity, particularly where twins are so similar in appearance as to be easily mistaken for one another. This argument would seem to be effectively countered by the following observation. If confusion of self-identity led to higher rates of concordance among identical twins, one would expect to find a higher risk of schizophrenia in identical twins than in the population as a whole. In fact, this is not the case.

Another explanation that has been advanced to account for the higher concordance in identical twin pairs than in fraternal pairs is that the former are exposed to more similar, predisposing environmental factors than the latter; that is to say that they are treated in such a way as to put pressure on them to behave alike. This hypothesis can be tested by looking at twin pairs separated at birth and raised in different environments; a high concordance rate for identical twins reared apart would refute the theory concerning the influence of this 'predisposing environment'. Seventeen such identical twin pairs have been studied in professional psychiatric literature, eleven of which (65 per cent) were concordant for schizophrenia.

These two examples are not intended to prove that twin studies are wholly without their methodological difficulties. On the whole, however, they provide persuasive evidence for the presence of a hereditary component in schizophrenia. This evidence is further strengthened by the results of complementary studies into the effects of adoption within families in which schizophrenia is by some means present.

Adoption studies

The pioneering work in the field of adoption studies was undertaken in Denmark and the United States. Dr Leonard Heston, now of the University of Washington, examined 47 children in Oregon who had been separated from their schizophrenic biological mothers within three days of birth and thereafter raised by adoptive parents with whom they had no biological relationship. Simultaneously, he studied a control group of 50 persons who had been separated from non-schizophrenic mothers. Both study groups were adults at the time of examination.

The idea behind this study was to discover whether children born to schizophrenic mothers would have a higher probability of becoming schizophrenic than children born to non-schizophrenic mothers, when no member of either group had been exposed to their mother or any other biological relation. If schizophrenia has a genetic cause, then the biological children of schizophrenic mothers should have a higher risk of developing the illness regardless of who raised them. If, in contrast, the parenting environment causes the illness, then separating children from a schizophrenic parent should prevent them from becoming schizophrenic themselves. Dr Heston's results found that five children of schizophrenic mothers became schizophrenic, whereas none of the children of non-schizophrenic mothers developed the illness. These results added to the accumulating evidence of a herditary basis for schizophrenia.

The Denmark studies, led by Dr Seymour Kety and colleagues from the United States National Institute of Mental Health, took advantage of a wealth of medical data and statistics in the Copenhagen area, where some 5500 children had been separated from their biological parents between 1923 and 1947. Of these children, 33 who later became schizophrenic were studied along with 33 non-schizophrenic adoptees selected for comparison. The investigators then examined the biological relatives of these schizophrenic and non-schizophrenic adoptees. To eliminate any possible bias in making diagnoses, all relatives studied did not know if they were linked with a schizophrenic or non-schizophrenic adoptee. The study diagnosed 21 per cent of the biological relations of schizophrenic individuals with schizophrenia or a related disorder, compared with 11 per cent of the biological relatives of non-schizophrenics. The study found no differences in rates of schizophrenia between the adoptive relatives of the schizophrenic and non-schizophrenic adoptees. Thus, the findings again provided strong evidence for a genetic basis for schizophrenia. Although the Danish study took a different perspective and starting point for its research from that of Dr Heston's US study, it too compared children born to schizophrenic families but raised by non-schizophrenic parents with those born to and raised by families untouched by the disease. Schizophrenia and related disorders were found in 32 per cent of the former group but only 18 per cent of the latter.

The studies discussed to this point clearly show that schizophrenic parents transmit the illness to their children even when those children are subsequently raised by non-schizophrenic parents. This in turn shows that biological relationships predict the risk for schizophrenia and may even suggest that parenting—the home environment in fact—is actually not significant.

Findings from the Danish studies thus strengthen the case for hereditary factors playing a major role in the transmission of schizophrenia. Adoption studies do, however, have their limitations. At this point in the debate, it was pointed out that even though an adopted child had been separated from its mother soon after birth, it had spent nine months in the mother's uterus before birth. During this period of time, a mother might transmit to a child, who would later be adopted, some form of non-genetic biological influence that would result in the child's developing schizophrenia fifteen years later.

What sort of factor could cause such delayed effects? One candidate among those who uphold this theory is a slow virus capable of lying dormant for many years before being triggered by a combination of biological and psychosocial conditions or stimuli. True, no such virus has been discovered; yet the possibility that one might exist could be seen as compromising the results of twin and adoption studies.

Fortunately for those who wished to uphold the integrity of such studies, the Danish researchers were able to examine the possibility of *in utero* transmission of schizophrenia. In their samples, there was a specific group of blood relatives who had not been exposed to the same uterine environment. These were half-brothers or sisters (from the father's side) of children who were given out for adoption and later developed schizophrenia. These paternal half-siblings have the same father, but different mothers. Kety and his colleagues found that 8 of 63 paternal half-siblings of schizophrenic adoptees (12.7 per cent) had schizophrenia when interviewed compared with only 1 of 64 paternal half-siblings of non-schizophrenic adoptees (1.6 per cent). Because paternal half-siblings have different mothers, these results cannot be explained by the *in utero* transmission of schizophrenia from mother to child. Indeed, a higher rate of schizophrenia was found among these half-siblings from the father's side than in the half-siblings of the control group. This fact provided the most compelling evidence for the hereditary basis of schizophrenia.

The Danish studies have subsequently been reproduced and replicated in a wider provincial Danish setting. Taken together with Heston's work on adoption, these projects motivated a concerted scientific effort to isolate and understand the mechanism by which schizophrenia was genetically transmitted in families. In turning to this subject, we must again consider some quite challenging scientific data. We cannot simply gloss over every complex aspect of the subject, for by doing so we would deprive the reader of the very 'facts' of schizophrenia that will ultimately prove most important in grasping its true nature. Equally importantly, it is in these fields that future researchers may well discover scientific techniques to relieve substantially, if not entirely eradicate schizophrenia. It would be a pity to deprive the reader of a working knowledge of these aspects of the illness, simply to produce a 'lighter' book now.

By what mechanism might schizophrenia be genetically transmitted?

Although family, twin, and adoption studies conclusively show that schizophrenia is at least partly an inherited condition, researchers have found it surprisingly difficult to identify the mechanism of genetic transmission. Several possibilities exist. At one extreme, it may be that an aberration in a single gene is responsible; at the other extreme, there may be many genes that act in concert with one another and with the environment to cause the illness.

The transmission of our genes obeys known biological laws that are mathematically describable. It ought, therefore, in theory to be possible to use the results of family, twin, and adoption studies to determine whether one, several, or very many genes are the cause of schizophrenia. Unfortunately, attempts to fit mathematical genetic models to schizophrenia studies have yielded contradictory results, some finding evidence to support the theory of single gene transmission, while others suggest that many genes must act in combination to produce the illness.

Rapid developments in the laboratory science of molecular genetics during the 1980s appeared at first to offer schizophrenia researchers the methodology they required to resolve this question. Specifically, a new technique for pinpointing specific genes know as **linkage analysis** seemed to make practicable what had for years been theoretically possible only. More encouragingly still, progress towards identifying the genetic basis of other diseases was swift, and our knowledge of the exact genes responsible for many serious complaints grows every year. The list already includes Huntingdon's disease (chorea), Alzheimer's disease, cystic fybrosis, Duchenne's muscular dystrophy and many more.

Linkage analysis in essence consists of first discovering pairs or sets of genes which owing to their proximity (linkage) on a chromosome are always passed down together in families. If, for example, one of these genes produces something readily observable such as a certain eye colour, and if this eye colour is consistently present in schizophrenic members of that family, it is theoretically acceptable to assume linkage and to proceed from there to further isolating the actual gene responsible for schizophrenia.

Sadly, this has not yet proved possible. A flurry of excitement occurred among the research community in the late 1980s, after several scientists seemed to find linkage between schizophrenia and genetic material on chromosome 5, but subsequent studies could not replicate their results.

What, then did these initial linkage analysis experiments add to our knowledge of schizophrenia? Apart from the lesson outlined above, they appeared to prove conclusively that schizophrenia, unlike say cystic fibrosis, is not a **simple** single gene disorder, where the pattern of transmission closely follows the laws of single gene inheritance. Rather, the mode of inheritance of schizophrenia is unknown and does not conform to such laws. In such cases, we describe the mode of inheritance as **complex**.

Evidence for another schizophrenia gene came from the efforts of Ann Pulver and collaborators at Johns Hopkins University, Baltimore. They identified a region on chromosome 22 that was linked to schizophrenia in a series of families. Similar findings were then reported by other investigators. Although there were some dissenting data, a collaborative analysis of eleven schizophrenia data sets led by Michael Gill of the Institute of Psychiatry in London supported Pulver's original finding. However, Dr Gill's analyses also suggested that the putative schizophrenia gene would account for no more than 2 per cent of the variability in the liability to develop the disorder.

A gene on chromosome 6 has also been implicated in schizophrenia. Kenneth Kendler of the Medical College of Virginia studied a series of schizophrenic families in Ireland. Linkage analyses of these families found fairly strong evidence for a schizophrenia gene on chromosome 6. However, like the chromosome 22 results, this finding could be replicated by some, but not all, investigators.

What are we to make of this inconsistent pattern of results? In our view, schizophrenia researchers appear to have found genes that exert a small effect on the onset of schizophrenia. Mutations in these genes may be crucial for a small subgroup, play a minor role in others, and be irrelevant to many more.

Nevertheless, the search for specific mutations that cause brain dysfunction and schizophrenia is now under-way. If specific mutations are discovered, they may help us to find other genes and will eventually lead to new treatments that target the genetic defects that lead to illness.

Setbacks such as those described above have not blunted the researchers' sense of enquiry, but rather pointed the way to the type of research necessary to progress our undestanding of this and similar conditions. In this case, future research for both geneticists and mental health researchers must focus on identifying the genes responsible for genetically complex illnesses.

Many such linkage studies of schizophrenia are now taking place. Since the basic material of such studies is the family unit, one of the many considerations these projects must address is that of precisely who is ill and who is not ill in the families being studied.

The quest to determine who, within a family group, is or is not suffering from schizophrenia is often a matter of distinguishing true schizophrenia from a variety of schizophrenia-like disorders which genetic research has shown us are probably caused by the same genes. These are known as 'schizophrenia spectrum disorders'.

Schizophrenia spectrum disorders

This is the collective term for these schizophrenia-like disorders, and the requirement for their identification is straightforward: to qualify, the disorder must affect the biological relatives of schizophrenic people more fre-quently than it affects those of people who are not schizophrenic.

Psychotic spectrum disorders

These disorders are very similar to schizophrenia but they do not meet the diagnostic criteria necessary to make the latter diagnosis. Two prominent examples are **schizoaffective disorder** and **psychosis not otherwise specified (NOS)**.

Schizoaffective disorder

As the name suggests, schizoaffective disorder is used to describe patients who exhibit features of both schizophrenia and affective (i.e. mood) disorders. The affective symptoms of these patients include depression, irritability, and mania, and will be equally prominent as their schizophrenic symptoms. In DSM-IV, the diagnosis of schizoaffective disorder requires that an episode of mood disorder be present for a substantial portion of the psychotic episode.

Psychosis NOS

Psychosis NOS is a 'residual' diagnostic category, that is to say one which is used to categorize patients who are clearly suffering a schizophrenia-like psychotic illness but do not fit into any of the rigorously defined categories for schizophrenia, schizoaffective disorder, or other well-defined psychotic conditions. Use of a residual category of this kind, rather than shoe-horning patients into categories where they do not exactly fit, serves to remind the clinician that more information needs to be gathered to achieve diagnostic certainty. In many cases, the psychosis NOS diagnosis is used as a temporary category for newly ill patients until the course of their symptoms reveals a more precise diagnosis.

We have said already that schizoaffective disorder and psychosis NOS are more common among the relatives of schizophrenics than those of non-schizophrenic people. Curiously, the former is also frequently found among the relatives of patients with bipolar (manic-depressive) disorder. This has led some investigators to conclude that schizophrenia and bipolar disorder may share genes in common. According to this view, the two illnesses lie at the extreme ends of a 'continuum of psychosis', and schizoaffective patients lie in the middle. This idea is controversial but deemed sufficiently worthy of further investigation because a good deal of research is currently devoted to it.

Schizotypal personality disorder

Psychiatrists have pondered the existence of mild forms of schizophrenia for nearly a century. Their observations of the relations of schizophrenic patients led them to note an uncommonly high proportion of 'eccentric personalities', poor social relationships, anxiety in social situations, and limited emotional responses among this group. The reader may recall that these symptoms are mild forms of the *negative* symptoms of schizophrenia. Less frequently, psychiatrists also found mild forms of *positive* symptoms within groups of relatives, including thought disorder, suspiciousness, illusions, and perceptual aberrations. These early observations by clinical researchers, in combination with systematic genetic studies, led to the creation of the diagnostic class now known as **schizotypal personality disorder**.

We all recognize that people's personalities, in common for example, with their intake of alcohol, vary greatly. Just as we define alcoholism according to whether people's drinking reaches levels where it causes distress to others and harm to themselves, so only when a person's personality is sufficiently troubled for it to make it hard for him to function normally would an 'eccentric' come to be seen as having a fully fledged personality disorder.

Schizotypal personality disorder is, in some ways, a mild form of schizophrenia, and the sufferer may experience the full range of schizophrenic symptoms, albeit in sufficiently diluted form to make normal life possible. For example, just as the schizophrenic may withdraw completely from society, the schizotypal patient may also be a pronounced 'loner', but one who is able to withstand human company when essential, and so never require hospital treatment.

The prevalence of schizotypal personality disorder among the relatives of schizophrenics has been documented by numerous family, adoption, and twin studies. Although not all have reached similar conclusions, there is general agreement that the biological relatives of schizophrenic patients demonstrate 'subthreshold' manifestations of the illness in the form of schizotypal personality disorder. The incidence of schizotypal personality among these relatives is between 4 and 15 per cent. If 'probable' cases are included, the rate may run as high as 27 per cent. A probable case is one that almost meets the diagnostic criteria for the disorder.

If the foregoing appears to convey the impression that families including one or more schizophrenic persons are likely to be riddled with eccentricity and even psychosis, it is worth remembering the distinction between increased risk and actuality. As a matter of fact, the typical schizophrenic is more likely than not to have no schizophrenic or schizotypal relatives.

We have seen that, at present (1997), researchers have not even isolated the genes responsible for typical schizophrenia; an equally daunting set of intellectual challenges awaits us as we move towards a consideration of the role of the environment in the contraction and course of the illness. There are no easy answers to any of the central questions of schizophrenia and we may be some years and much research away from unquestionable conclusions to even the most simple among them.

8 How does the environment affect schizophrenia?

Another word about definitions

'When *I* use a word,' Humpty Dumpty said, in a rather scornful voice, 'it means just what I choose it to mean— neither more nor less.'

Lewis Carroll: *Through the looking glass.* 1871

The reader will rapidly become aware that virtually every section of this book begins with an exploration of the definition of a term or terms to be employed in it. It is not our intention to appear pedantic, but it is occasionally essential to pause and compare the everyday use of a word with the way in which it is used in psychiatric study.

A scientific term, with all due deference to Humpty Dumpty, means exactly what the scientific community has decreed it to mean—no more and no less. If a specific term must occur four or five times in one paragraph, then we sacrifice elegance of style for precision of meaning.

What is meant by the term 'environment'?

Environment is a perfect example of a word that has a multiplicity of meanings and shades of meaning in common language. In ordinary speech, the word, when used alone, is usually employed to mean 'family upbringing' or 'the world's ecosystem'. It can, however, be used to denote more specific areas or sets of circumstances: 'salmon thrive well in this environment', for example.

For the purpose of this section, which deals with some of the environmental factors which might cause or modify schizophrenia, an **environmental factor** should be taken to mean: *any event not due to the genes carried by the father's sperm and the mother's egg before conception.* These events may be biological (e.g. head injuries, viral infections), psychological (e.g. disrupted family relationships), or social (e.g. poverty).

The distinction between **causes** and **modifiers** of schizophrenia is crucial to this subject. In this book we use the term **cause** to refer to any agent which can produce the illness in anyone who has not and has never been ill with schizophrenia. To employ a philosophical distinction, this cause does not have to be either *necessary* (that is to say that it *must* be present for the illness to occur) or *sufficient* (meaning that its presence *alone* will cause the illness). In practice, this means, respectively, that other causes may exist that also produce the illness and that the putative cause may require other causes to be present for the illness to occur.

The term **modifier** is used to refer to any agent that changes the clinical presentation of the illness in someone who is already sick. As we shall discuss in the following subsection, knowledge of modifiers can help considerably with the treatment of the disorder. They should not, however, be mistaken for causes.

Do environmental factors cause schizophrenia?

Scientists long ago realized that the transmission of schizophrenia is neither wholly due to 'nature' (genetics) nor 'nurture' (environment). Indeed, the twin studies we have already considered proved this conclusively by showing that even pairs with the same genes only contracted the illness 50 per cent of the time. Clearly, some environmental influence or 'trigger' is required to activate the illness.

Environmental influences may be amenable to change and might, therefore, offer us hope of treatments for the condition. If, for example, we knew that poverty or bad housing caused schizophrenia, then public development programmes could be established with the goal of preventing the illness. Having said in the earlier part of this section that the term **environment** must be understood in its broadest possible sense when discussing schizophrenia and other mental illnesses, research has in fact concentrated on several quite specific aspects of environment, namely:

(1) family relationships;

(2) social environment;

(3) socioeconomic status;

(4) schizophrenia as a symptom of a sick society;

(5) biological factors.

A detailed examination of these factors, considered as possible causes or modifiers of schizophrenia, is far beyond the realistic scope of this book. Some consideration must, nonetheless, be given to each, even at the risk of exposing the reader to more relatively 'dry' scientific data.

Family relationships

Although, as we have shown, **environment** is an extremely inclusive term in psychiatric research, clinicians have tended to concentrate on the family unit as the most potentially influential factor in the causation or modification of the illness. Indeed, for the first two-thirds of the century, the mental health professions were dominated by theorists and researchers who believed that most mental illness was caused by events that interrupted, delayed, or otherwise disrupted psychological development. This assumed, the family seemed the most logical focal point for research into the cause of schizophrenia.

Unfortunately, many of these theories, although apparently backed up by observation and anecdotal evidence, amounted to little more than speculation, hypothesis, or opinion. It is worth spending a little time to consider some of the more serious of these misconceptions.

Schizophrenogenic mothers

One of the most invidious concepts to be introduced into the debate on the origins of schizophrenia is that of the *schizophrenogenic mother*. Roughly expressed, this theory states that some mothers, by their very style of raising their children, greatly increase the likelihood of them developing the disease. Such mothers, it is claimed, send out contradictory and confusing signals regarding correct behaviour; convey and hence encourage inconsistent emotional responses; are overprotective of their children and insensitive to their psychological and affective needs. Presented with these psychological conundrums, the child's response is to retreat into a fantasy world. When 'properly' interpreted, however, this retreat turns out to be an entirely reasonable strategy for coping with the dysfunctional environment he is forced to inhabit. Psychiatrists—seldom greatly admired by those who uphold such theories—are little more than pseudo-scientists who, for an appropriate fee, will confer the status of *illness* on this situation, thus absolving the parent from responsibility, and (usually) proceed to drug the sufferer into a less troublesome state.

Why do we describe the concept of the schizophrenogenic mother as invidious?

We do this in part because if you are reading this book as the parent of a schizophrenic child, you may well have encountered the theory before and consequently suffered feelings of responsibility, if not outright guilt for your child's illness. Although it is true that some families appear to include parents whose attitude and behaviour did little to help their schizophrenic offspring, we feel that it is irresponsible to extrapolate from those observations an entire theory that blames parents for the development of the illness in their children.

We have already discussed the prevalence of schizo-affective and schizotypal personalities within families with one schizophrenic member, and there will obviously be cases where the parents of schizophrenic children suffer from one of these conditions. In noting this, however, we do not imply—and it should not be inferred—that their behaviour necessarily affects for the worse that of their schizophrenic children.

Later in the book we do consider the ways in which families—and parents in particular—can help or hinder the schizophrenic person, so we are by no means discounting the importance of family interaction to the **course** of the illness (i.e. the pattern that its symptoms and periods of remission will take through the sufferer's life). There are, however, well-founded intellectual reasons for discarding much of the evidence for the theory of the existence of the schizophrenogenic mother.

First, there is the ancient dilemma of the chicken and the egg—which came first? The theory does not take into account the possibility that the so-called schizo-phrenogenic mother's behaviour and attitudes may develop as a consequence of having a schizophrenic child. Even if it could be shown that the mother had certain personality traits before the onset of her child's schizophrenia, it is possible that abnormal or socially deviant characteristics of the pre-schizophrenic child might have served to create these traits.

There is also another possibility. The mothers of schizophrenic children may have passed the schizo-phrenia gene to their child. In other words, the mother may be an undiagnosed schizophrenic, or someone suffering a schizophrenia-like illness which expresses itself in traits such as overprotectiveness or hostility. Thus, any so-called 'schizophrenogenic' characteristics may also be caused by the genetic cause of schizophrenia.

Finally, one must consider the strain to parents of rearing and looking after schizophrenic children, which may continue until the parent is quite elderly, and the distress of seeing one's loved ones robbed by the illness of much of the happiness and satisfaction offered by a 'normal, happy life'. Nor should it be forgotten that very elderly parents with acutely sick children may, depending on the quality of mental health care available at the time and place, have ample reason to worry about the future their offspring will have to face without them.

Double-bind theory

Mothers or mothers-to-be reading this book may be wondering whether the fathers of schizophrenics have been accorded the same interest. If the parent–child relationship is important, then surely the father's personality should also be studied. In fact, fathers were included in another hypothesis that implicated a particular type of abnormal communication between either parent and their child, the so-called *double-bind* situation. In double-bind communication, the child is repeatedly exposed to contradictory messages. These may be communicated by the same parent at different times, or by the two parents giving separate, and contradictory, advice, instructions, or commands. For example, the father or mother might tell the child that she may leave the house, but simultaneously forbid her to do so by exhibiting prohibitory non-verbal signals. Hence, the parent's verbal message requires one response, whereas another form of communication demands the opposite.

This theory of schizophrenia appeared to explain some of the behaviour of schizophrenic patients. The study group which produced the results was, however, small, and the evidence of broader, well-designed experiments has since rendered it suspect.

Parents' marital relationships

It has also been postulated that children observing highly abnormal or irrational behaviour within their parents' marriage might respond by becoming schizophrenic. Studies focused on two forms of abnormal marriage. In the **skewed** relationship, a passive parent yielded control of the family to an abnormal partner (usually female), who subsequently turned her destructive attentions on the (usually male) child.

The second type of abnormal family relationship was termed **marital schism**, and was characterized by parents in chronic conflict. Each ignored mutual needs to pursue separate goals and in the process competed for the child's support. Proponents of this theory claimed that marital schism was common between the parents of female schizophrenics.

As with the idea of marital skew, marital schism has been clearly shown by subsequent research to exercise no calculable effect on schizophrenic children. We can safely conclude that abnormal parental relationships do not cause schizophrenia.

Disordered family communication

A greater degree of credence has been given to the idea of disordered family communication causing schizophrenia, with an appropriately greater degree of specialist research devoted to its central hypothesis. Research conducted in the United States about two decades ago made intensive studies of the communication styles of four families, each containing a schizophrenic member. The results identified two common forms of disordered communication: the first was **amorphous thinking**, characterized by vague ideas and unclear reasoning; the second was **fragmented thinking** in which thoughts were clear but disjointed from each other with weak links between ideas.

This theory, after promising results from early research, was ultimately to prove as untenable as the others.

Whatever anecdotal evidence might suggest, the way in which families communicate cannot be proved to cause schizophrenia.

Social environment

We have already noted that studies conducted in different countries have occasionally produced significantly different prevalence rates for schizophrenia, even when every reasonable step has been taken to ensure congruence between methodologies, diagnostic definitions, sizes of sample, and so on. What can account for these cross-cultural differences?

Two extremes of prevalence rate were reported after studies into a small community in northern Sweden on the one hand and into the Hutterite people of North America on the other. The prevalence was 10.8 per 1000 in the former and 1.1 per 1000 in the latter. Such differences led some researchers to postulate that sociocultural aspects of environment might cause schizophrenia.

In fact, the differences are more likely to be due to social selection. We have already seen that schizophrenic sufferers tend to shun social interaction, often to the point of living as hermits. When one examines the two communities studied, this factor becomes critical. The Hutterites are a North American Anabaptist religious sect, and their community is notably close knit. The probable explanation for the low prevalence of schizophrenia among them is that any of their members with schizophrenic traits would tend to move out in order to avoid the high degree of social interaction demanded by his peers.

Northern Sweden, in contrast, is a sparsely populated area where the climate is severe and people lead extremely isolated lives. Such a social environment, although uncongenial in the extreme to most people, might be highly appealing to a schizophrenic. A high frequency of cousin marriages was also found in this as in many isolated areas, and such intermarriage within a population already carrying the genes for schizophrenia would further increase the high number of sufferers found there.

Socioeconomic status

People in the lower social classes face numerous disadvantages in areas that research has conclusively linked to health problems in general. Poverty, malnutrition, poor prenatal care of mothers, poor medical care in countries without free state provision, and disordered family situations make up only a partial list. Clearly, it is reasonable to suggest that such factors will lead to an increased risk of mental illness.

Consequently, epidemiological researchers were not surprised to find higher admission rates for schizophrenia among inner-city, low social class dwellers, in both Europe and America. Some went on to conclude that highly disadvantageous socioeconomic circumstances could cause schizophrenia.

With this proposition, we return reluctantly to the chicken and the egg, for is not schizophrenia equally likely to *cause* low social status as to result from it? We shall look in greater depth at the social problems faced by schizophrenics in a later section of this book, but expressed briefly, schizophrenics are less likely to have work (and hence money), secure housing, and the support of a community of friends and relatives. They are, therefore, prone to 'downward social drift' in much the same way as alcoholics of high social status may literally be brought to the point of living rough on the streets.

We do not need to present a detailed account of the ways by which researchers have approached the problem of disproving that social adversity alone could cause schizophrenia.

Briefly, however, it was first established that an element of downward drift *did* occur, with young schizophrenics exhibiting lower social status than their parents at a similar age. Since a comparison of the social status of the fathers themselves revealed no significant differences, it was concluded that their children's downward drift was the result of their illness.

A second strand of research concentrated on ethnic groups. A recent study by Dr Bruce Dohrenwend of Columbia University provides additional evidence that low social class does not cause schizophrenia. His studies concentrated on ethnic minority groups and were based on the premise that since racial discrimination is a form of social adversity, minorities should be at *greater risk* for schizophrenia than non-minorities. If, in contrast, it is schizophrenia that causes downward social drift, the minorities should have a lower risk of the illness, since many who are healthy, talented, and capable of achievement would be artificially 'held back' by the discrimination inherent in society.

The most notable conclusion of these studies was to confirm the risk of downward social drift among schizophrenic men. This risk for members of the low-status social groups studied was 4 per cent among non-minority members and 2 per cent among minority individuals. In short, it can be taken that schizophrenia causes people to have a lower social class, rather than vice versa.

The degree to which those who are sick, particularly in the inner cities, may go untreated and uncared for is just one example of the many injustices in our society. But could we go far enough as to say that it is society that is 'sick' and schizophrenia is a 'symptom' of its disease?

Schizophrenia as a symptom of a sick society

Sometimes in life, situations develop that only the half-crazy can get out of.

La Rochefoucauld: *Maxims.* 1665

A minority of mental health practitioners argue that schizophrenia is a symptom of a sick society, and that the pressures exerted on families drive them to single out a member to bear the burden. Moreover, those we diagnose as having the 'illness' are actually undergoing a therapeutic experience which will help them to recover from this sickness refreshed.

It is worth noting that such theorists do not confine the sickness in society to particular quarters or social classes; everyone has the potential to fall sick. Stated like this, the theory may well appear palpable nonsense. And yet still more extreme theories have enjoyed periods of vogue, during which the thinking public have been encouraged to view society as so pathologically corrupt that certain forms of insanity will in due course become the only rational means of facing the conflicting and alienating forces at large in our communities.

Foremost among these theorists is (or, more accurately, until recently *was*) Thomas Szasz, hailed in the early 1960s as 'the father of modern anti-psychiatry'. His books, which bore self-explanatory titles like *The manufacture of madness* and *The myth of mental illness* were widely read by students of disciplines as wide ranging as philosophy, sociology, or social history and psychology. Szasz is a persuasive arguer, who uses genuinely powerful but often far from representative data and examples to draw his readers along with him.

Undeniably, there have been, as Szasz points out repeatedly, periods of history and political regimes in which the definitions of sanity or madness have become the province of society as embodied in the state, rather than of unbiased specialists whose first commitment is to the patient. The former Soviet Union used state power and force to decree that political unorthodoxy is psychiatrically pathological. One might fairly say that the former Soviet Union was 'sick' with paranoia during periods of its history. During these times, the climate of fear and suspicion and the understandable political reticence of most citizens became so much the norm that an individual who openly questioned the prevailing political ideologies was diagnosed as 'mentally ill' and confined to institutions at which he could be 're-educated'.

The books written by those who view society as sufficiently sick to cause schizophrenia among some of its members, and psychiatry as little more than a parasitic pseudo-science, can be stimulating and thought-provoking to read. Certainly, they are likely to be better company on a long flight than the average psychiatry textbook. They do not, however, always reflect modern psychiatry entirely truthfully nor, more importantly, do they offer much practical help for those concerned with the treatment of mental illness. Improvements in the quality of this treatment may involve considerable societal change; whether such improvements would restore us to 'sanity', depends on the way one views society in the first place.

Biological factors

During the past three decades, scientists have progressively shifted the focus of their research away from family relationships and the social environment. Instead, increasing attention has been paid to environmental events that have biological significance for the developing human brain.

It is important for the reader to understand that these events are called **biological** as opposed to **psychological** or **social** because they are known to disturb biological functioning. A head injury capable of causing brain damage would be one example; where schizophrenia is concerned, the principal events upon which research has concentrated are complications in pregnancy or delivery, and viruses.

Pregnancy and delivery complications

Any event that affects the fetus in the mother's uterus is classified as a **prenatal** event. These include physical trauma, malnutrition, infection, and intoxication. Those occurring at the time of birth are termed **perinatal**. Events such as physical injury, lack of oxygen, infection, and bleeding would fall into this class. Events that occur after birth, whether biological or psychosocial, are called **postnatal**. When postnatal events occur close to the time of birth, they are included with pre- and perinatal events under the term **pregnancy and delivery complications**, or **PDC**s for convenience.

Many studies have found increased rates of PDCs in the births of children who have eventually become schizophrenic. Although these rates were deemed noteworthy, they were not especially pronounced when considered beside the figure for the general population. The great majority of babies who experienced PDCs did not become schizophrenic. However, when researchers considered the PDC study results in combination with those of genetic studies, a simple yet powerful hypothesis emerged. It appeared that the effect of PDCs was to trigger schizophrenia in those babies who, by dint of their genetic heritage were predisposed to schizophrenia. This is sometimes known as the **diathesis–stress theory** because it requires a predisposition (diathesis) and an adverse event (stress) for the illness to develop.

Further research strongly suggested that PDCs were predictive of later schizophrenia and schizotypal personality. There are, however, other theories that PDCs cause a non-genetic form of schizophrenia. Although some research has found PDCs among patients with no family history of the illness, at the time of writing (1997), there is no adequate way of interpreting the contradictory data obtained by these studies.

The viral hypothesis

Viruses, as we know, are capable of causing illnesses ranging in severity from mild colds to AIDS. It is not, therefore, unreasonable that they might have the potential to cause a condition such as schizophrenia.

The main epidemiological basis for this theory rests on the observation that the births of schizophrenic children are more likely to occur during the late winter and spring months than at other times of the year. Children born during these months are at increased risk of exposure to viruses while they are in the womb. This **season of birth effect** has been studied with interesting, if not entirely consistent results, but it cannot alone be deemed to prove the viral hypothesis.

If schizophrenia were caused by the action of a virus on the brain of a developing fetus, we would expect to observe other effects or 'symptoms' in the individual concerned. Two such effects *have* been noted in schizophrenia: sufferers exhibit elevated rates of physical abnormality such as facial deformities, and abnormal dermatoglyphic patterns (fingerprints). Both of these could, it is true, equally be caused by PDCs or genetic abnormalities, but their presence in schizophrenia is consistent with the action of a virus. Once again, such research as has been conducted into the viral hypothesis has thus far proved inconclusive; we await the 'breakthrough' study or experiment which will decide the matter beyond doubt.

Sporadic and familial schizophrenia

Some studies of biological environmental factors have posited the existence of **sporadic schizophrenia**. The term is used to refer to cases that do not have their origins within the family. **Familial schizophrenia**, in contrast, refers to cases of the illness that occur with other cases in the family. The word 'familial' is chosen over 'genetic' because an illness may cluster in families for non-genetic reasons. That said, we believe that most cases of familial schizophrenia are indeed of a genetic origin.

We can distinguish between sporadic and familial cases of the illness simply: patients having one or more schizophrenic relative(s) are familial; those with no ill relatives are sporadic. They do not differ significantly according to any of the usual indicators—age, sex, and, so on—or in most of the clinical aspects of their condition. There are, however, differences in brain functioning. Most notably, familial schizophrenics are more likely to have problems with attention span; they find it difficult to perform tasks that require them to focus on an object at length, and they are more easily distractible and diverted away from a set activity. When examined by sophisticated methods, such as computerized axial tomography (CAT) scans or magnetic resonance imaging (MRI) that produce images of the brain's structure, sporadic schizophrenics show evidence of atrophy (shrinking) or loss of brain cells. Pregnancy and delivery complications and winter births also tend to be common among this group in comparison with familial schizophrenics.

It should be noted that not every study has supported these conclusions, and the competing diathesis–stress theory cannot be wholly ruled out. Nonetheless, the available results tend to support the theory that environmental events like viruses or PDCs can produce brain damage which could lead to a non-genetic form of schizophrenia or a form that requires fewer genes than does familial schizophrenia.

Do environmental factors affect the course of schizophrenia?

Until now, we have been concerned with the environment only as a potential *causal* agent in schizophrenia. What of the 'weaker' theory that the environment may *modify the course of the illness*, irrespective of its ultimate cause? In medical terminology, the course of an illness is the degree to which its symptoms wax and wane over time.

Schizophrenia has a highly variable course; some patients are virtually never free from symptoms, whereas others have periodic episodes of the illness, punctuated by periods of lucidity during which they are capable of leading an active, 'normal' life.

As we said earlier, the environment, unlike genetic inheritance, can be manipulated in a variety of ways. If research supports the hypothesis that the environment plays a significant role in modifying the course of this illness, we shall have discovered something concrete that can be done to ameliorate its effects on the sufferer. Certainly, the knowledge accumulated so far suggests that this is the case. We know that people are treated for schizophrenia, and, given the highly inclusive medical definition of the term 'environment', common sense suggests that any postnatal treatment is, by definition, tantamount to manipulation of their environment. Why would this be done if it has no effect on the course of the illness?

Much of the remainder of the book deals with the ways in which the psychiatric and caring professions attempt to improve the biological and psychosocial environments of schizophrenics. In this section, however, we are still concerned with the issue of how and if the central questions of schizophrenia have been approached by researchers, and we must briefly address the studies of environmental influences which initially led to the relevant conclusions.

Research has, in the main, concentrated on two kinds of environmental factors, namely those likely to affect the individual's ability to 'cope' and those which are likely to be most commonly associated with day-to-day emotional outlook. In practice, this has meant examining the effects of *stressful life events* and *family and social environments*.

To summarize the results of this research, it is fair to say that they were as positive as the unavoidable imprecision of language and concepts, such as *marital breakdown* or *stressful working conditions*, can permit.

Sufficient correlation was found between the occurrence of stressful life events and noxious or disordered family relationships and a worsening of symptoms and likelihood of relapse, respectively. We shall have cause to look again at both these subjects in the context of treating and coping with schizophrenia, at which point we hope to offer some guidance to those living close to sufferers on how best to avoid adverse environmental stimuli and manage with those that cannot be avoided.

Is schizophrenia a disease of the brain?

In the traditional language of medicine, disorders that alter the functioning of the psychological or emotional processes are classified as either **symptomatic** or **idiopathic**. **Symptomatic disorders** are those for which there is a known physical cause. For example, temporal lobe epilepsy, strokes, and brain tumours can lead to disturbed mental functioning and emotional expression. An **idiopathic disorder**, in contrast, has no known physical cause. The word *known* is emphasized because most scientists believe that a physical cause of schizophrenia will one day be discovered. In a former usage, **idiopathic** meant that these disorders were due to psychological and social events that had no physical effects on the brain.

The past fifteen years have seen a revolution in the psychiatric approach to mental illness generally, and to schizophrenia in particular. Many scientists and clinicians began to question the belief, advanced in its extreme form by Laing and his followers in the 1960s, that schizophrenia was rooted in psychological and family conflict. Instead, they surmised that the massive alterations in thought and emotion afflicting the schizophrenic patient were caused by a disease of the brain.

This biological revolution in psychiatry was fuelled by a variety of findings. We have already, for example, presented evidence that the causes of schizophrenia are at least in part genetic. Since genes regulate biological processes including brain function, this evidence strengthens biological theories of schizophrenia; also, research into environmental factors indicates a role for those that have a clear biological impact on the brain. Psychological and social events, albeit important as modifiers of the course of the illness, do not appear to play a prominent causal role.

In this chapter, we are concerned with one simple proposition, namely that biological processes are disrupted in the brains of schizophrenic people. The scientific methodologies employed to test this theory and the terminology in which their results are expressed, are far from simple. Scientists working in this field have applied virtually every new neurodiagnostic technology to the problem and while we shall make every attempt to avoid the use of over-technical language, certain new terms and concepts must be employed and understood.

Two such terms are **aetiology** and **pathophysiology**. The former refers to the causes of brain dysfunction, and the latter to the specific modifications of the brain that led to the illness. For example, a mutation in a gene controlling brain cell physiology might be the aetiology of schizophrenia; the corresponding pathophysiology might be atrophy of the brain as revealed by a brain scan.

Structural brain abnormalities

This phrase is used to denote any unusual changes in the form or configuration of the brain observed in schizophrenic, but not in healthy people. Post-mortem studies of donated brains have revealed that abnormalities are common among schizophrenics. Equally important, researchers have discovered no single abnormality in all or even most of the brains studied. This is a highly curious result; most well-defined brain diseases leave a common 'signature' on the brain; schizophrenia can, it appears, cause a wide variety of structural brain abnormalities.

Evidence of this form is today amassed by use of brain imaging technology—a type of X-ray of the living brain. As early as 1927, however, a form of imaging did exist with the impressive title, **pneumono-encephalography**. When used to examine schizophrenic brains, this technique found that 18 out of 19 schizophrenics had enlarged ventricles. These are spaces within the brain containing fluid, but not solid brain substance. When the brain substance surrounding them atrophies, the ventricles enlarge. The overall result is a smaller, lighter brain with fewer cells. Unfortunately, this early finding, although confirmed in subsequent experiments, did not fit the prevailing theories of schizophrenia and was hence discarded by the scientific community.

Psychiatry rediscovered brain atrophy in 1976 when Eva Johnstone (now at Edinburgh University), Timothy Crow (now at Oxford University) and colleagues at the British Medical Research Council Clinical Research Centre reported ventricular enlargement in schizophrenic patients evaluated with the CAT and MRI scanning techniques described in the previous chapter. These techniques confirmed that schizophrenics may suffer enlarged ventricles and reduced brain tissue volumes, respectively. Significant as this research has proven, it has thrown up as many questions as it has answered. The most problematic of these follows from the fact that although as a group schizophrenics have larger ventricles than is normal, many schizophrenic individuals have normal-sized ventricles. Indeed, depending on the group studied, anywhere between 20 and 50 per cent will exhibit this syndrome.

Patients with enlarged ventricles tend to have more negative symptoms such as flattening of affect (emotional blunting), more pronounced difficulties with thinking, and are generally more seriously affected by the illness, necessitating longer-term care and a carefully structured living environment. Despite these findings, attempts to identify ventricular enlargement with a specific subtype of schizophrenia have so far proved inconclusive. To complicate the picture further, enlargement of the ventricles is not confined to schizophrenia. It has also been reported in other psychiatric illnesses including bipolar disorder, schizoaffective disorder, and obsessive–compulsive disorder.

Abnormalities in brain functioning

Whereas studies of brain structure investigate the physical form and configuration of the brain, those of brain functioning are concerned with whether the organ is working correctly, regardless of its overall form and the configuration of its parts.

A simple example should serve to clarify the distinction between brain structure and function. Consider a car that will not start. If a part, say the battery, is missing, we conclude that the structure of the engine is abnormal. In contrast, if the battery is weak and the spark plugs dirty, we conclude that despite its normal structure, the engine has two specific defects in functioning.

Unfortunately, we cannot employ many easily understood similes of this type when considering complex aspects of the brain. It may be worth reminding ourselves at this point that this book does not claim to be a specialist text, but rather a general introduction to the subject of schizophrenia. The reader wishing to pursue an advanced study into the scientific aspects of the illness will find no shortage of appropriate literature in print. This varies from professional papers covering highly specific aspects of schizophrenia, to more comprehensive textbooks on mental illness generally intended for the professional psychiatrist or advanced student of the subject.

Rather than attempt a detailed presentation of the facts of brain functioning, we have elected to err on the side of brevity and simplicity. We have, therefore, included only those points that the reader is likely to remember and which will genuinely help one to understand schizophrenia better.

Physiological measures of brain functioning

The development of new technologies that permit researchers to examine the living brain without harming the subject, have been crucial to the progress of our understanding of the condition. Foremost among these technologies are the CAT and MRI imaging techniques already described and the regional cerebral blood flow (RCBF) and positron emission tomography (PET) methods that measure blood flow to, and metabolism of glucose in, specific areas of the brain, respectively.

Both RCBF and PET studies confirm a relative reduction in metabolic activity in the frontal cortex of the brain in the case of schizophrenics. This area of the brain is responsible for many aspects of thought and emotion, and it co-ordinates and integrates the activities of other brain centres. The reductions have been most notable when the patient has performed a mental task during the procedure, suggesting that the schizophrenic brain cannot react to the world around it as quickly or efficiently as a healthy brain.

Another theory proposes that the left temporal lobe of the brain is dysfunctional in schizophrenics. This seems to be suggested by the observation that temporal lobe epilepsy, which affects only the left lobe of the brain, produces many schizophrenia-like symptoms. A little more support for the theory has been provided by evidence of the high proportion of left-handed people among schizophrenics. Most people are right-handed because the left side of their brain is dominant to their right. Since the left side of the brain controls the right hand (and vice versa), left-handedness may indicate that the left side of the brain has lost its dominance over the right side. This idea has received much attention because the left side of the brain is usually regarded as controlling language and thought, both of which are notably impaired in schizophrenia.

Overall, the theories that schizophrenics have impaired frontal cortex and left brain functions is supported by RCBF and PET studies, as it is by the older electroencephalogram (EEG) and the more recently developed brain potential imaging (BPI) technique.

Clearly, the schizophrenic brain does not function normally. What the physiological studies described above do not tell us, however, is how these abnormalities affect behaviour. In approaching this issue, we are moving into a subspeciality of psychology, known as **neuropsychology**.

Neuropsychological measures of brain functioning

The basis of neuropsychological research consists of monitoring the patient as he performs a variety of tasks designed to measure specific aspects of brain functioning. To test verbal memory, the patient is told a story and then asked questions about it, to see if key points have been remembered. To test visual memory, one shows the patient designs which he is then asked to recall. A summary of the results of a series of tests shows that schizophrenics display marked difficulties when compared with the performance of 'healthy' people tested as a 'control' experiment. To mention just some of these, schizophrenic patients exhibit poor performance in the following areas: short-term focusing on a task (**immediate attention**); concentrating on a task for a long space of time (**sustained attention**); and focusing on one thing while ignoring another in the background (**selective attention**).

Motor ability refers to the co-ordination of thought and muscle action to accomplish a task. One important aspect of normal motor function is speed. In most studies, schizophrenics are consistently slower to accomplish tasks than healthy subjects. Whether this slowness is associated with poor attention or lack of other abilities, the patient's slow responses are likely to impair significantly the patient's chances of employment.

The schizophrenic also exhibits marked difficulties with higher-level thought processes such as **abstraction** and **concept formation**. The former involves moving from the specific, observable aspects of life to general principles, while the latter describes the formation of categories and general groupings. The poor performance of schizophrenics at these tasks is related to reduced activity in the frontal cortex of the brain. Hence, we can see that the neuropsychological studies are consistent with the imaging studies discussed earlier.

When we discussed the symptoms of schizophrenia in Section One of this book, we looked in some detail at the phenomenon of thought disorder. It will not, therefore, surprise the reader to learn that the same patients exhibit neuropsychological deficiencies with verbal ability and language, learning, and memory. They fare better, however, on visual–spatial tasks, such as memorizing and reproducing specified patterns, object shapes, or forms. Why should this be? The answer probably lies in the domain of *brain asymmetry*. Put very simply, this refers to the fact that although the brain is physically symmetrical (i.e. if cut in half, the left and right portions look very similar to one another), it is functionally asymmetrical. It may well be that the defects that tend to affect the schizophrenic brain largely bypass the areas responsible for visual–spatial thinking, concentrating instead on those governing thought and language. Indeed, this is consistent with our structural discoveries regarding the concentration of dysfunction in the left side, rather than the right side of the brain.

What causes these dysfunctions?

We have now noted many of the structural and functional malfunctions common to the schizophrenic brain, as revealed by brain imaging technology and neuropsychological research. But are we any nearer to finding a cause for them or, for that matter, for schizophrenia in general?

Research into schizophrenia is often frustratingly inconclusive; again and again we progress from observed trends to explanatory hypothesis, and undertake complex and painstaking research, only to discover so many exceptions to our putative 'rule' that we must dilute our conclusions to 'probability statements'.

This is not, of course, to decry the validity or importance of this research. If progress has been slow, this is simply a measure of the extreme complexity of the illness. In the following pages, we shall effectively bring the reader up to date with the current state of neurological research into schizophrenia by briefly describing the mechanism which many psychiatrists believe is responsible for the dysfunctions already depicted.

Neurotransmitter dysfunction

To know the cause of brain dysfunction in schizophrenia is to identify the ultimate cause of the illness. Many scientists have proposed that this lies within the **neurotransmitter systems** of the brain. To examine their theories, we must first provide a simple overview of how these systems work.

The brain is composed of thousands of brain cells called **neurones**. Some neurones collect information from the five senses and relay it to neurones in other areas of the brain for mental processing. These may in turn relay it to yet others for further processing. To relay information, neurones pass chemical messages across a small gap called a **synapse**. The chemical, known as a **neurotransmitter**, lands on a platform or **receptor**, on the second neurone, specially designed to permit it to bind on to its host. When sufficient receptors are occupied, an electronic impulse is created in the second neurone. When this tiny electrical charge reaches sufficient intensity, a 'message', specific to that neurotransmitter is sent across the second neurone. In this way, neurones in the brain communicate with one another and control the functions of mind and body.

This remarkable system is every bit as delicately balanced as common sense would suggest, and diseases can interfere with its normal operation in a number of ways. The first neurone may not produce enough chemical, it may produce too much, or produce the wrong chemical; the second neurone may not have enough receptors or it may have too many; the receptor may be wrongly shaped, preventing the neurotransmitter from landing and binding to it.

We already know that many mental illnesses are caused by malfunctions in this chemical system within the brain. Many researchers believe that imbalances in the concentration of neurotransmitters or abnormal activities at the synapse may cause schizophrenia. These theories are best approached by consideration of the various neurotransmitters commonly implicated in the condition.

Dopamine

This is the most studied neurotransmitter in schizophrenia research. Initially, interest in this particular chemical was aroused by observations of psychosis caused by the use of amphetamine, a drug which stimulates the brain's dopamine production, and causes symptoms indistinguishable from those of schizophrenia.

It has also been discovered that a group of medicines called **neuroleptics**, about which we shall have more to say when we look at the treatment of schizophrenia, are able to reduce these symptoms, whether caused by amphetamine abuse or schizophrenia itself. Although much remains to be discovered about the exact mechanism by which these drugs work, it seems most likely that they block dopamine receptors, preventing dopamine from landing and the corresponding message being sent.

Put simply, the dopamine theory of schizophrenia says that the dopamine circuits in the brain are overloaded.

Symptoms of incorrect dopamine message interpretation include hearing voices and maintaining bizarre beliefs that are unsupported by fact. Having said this, a causal connection between dopamine and schizophrenia has not been proven beyond doubt, and we hesitate to conclude that it could be considered a single cause of the illness.

Further post-mortem examination of schizophrenic brains would greatly help clarify this hypothesis. In 1978, Dr Timothy Crow lead a group of investigators whose research reported a significant increase in the average number of dopamine receptors in schizophrenic brains which, they concluded, resulted in the overloading of the dopamine circuit. Neuroleptics, Crow claimed, work because they block the excess platforms until only the correct number of messages reach the receiving neurone.

The problem with this hypothesis, like so many arguments relating to the aetiology of schizophrenia, is that the phenomenon is not observed in *all* patients; indeed, only about two-thirds of schizophrenics have increased numbers of dopamine receptors. The phenomenon cannot then, strictly, stand as a necessary cause of the illness.

One further theory proposes that positive symptoms of schizophrenia are caused by excessive dopamine activity, whereas negative symptoms are caused by its longer-term breakdown into other chemicals that are harmful to the brain. With the mechanism by which these toxins would normally be removed from the brain impaired, they are left to destroy or 'burn out' dopamine pathways in some areas of the brain. A 'pathway' can be envisaged as the route to or from other neurone areas with which dopamine must communicate by sending their electronic messages across the synapse.

Other neurochemical systems

The perceived failure of dopamine to identify conclusively the cause of schizophrenia motivated a wider examination of neurochemical systems within the brain.

The size and scope of this book prevents us from review-ing these researches comprehensively, but we shall pre-sent a representative sample of them.

A relation of dopamine, known as **tyrosine hydroxy-lase** was also implicated in the cause of schizophrenia after researchers noted that medicines which inhibit or reduce its chemical action also alleviate certain symptoms of the illness. Moreover, high levels of this chemical have been found in the brains of deceased schizophrenics. The relationship of the two chemicals is such that an excess of tyrosine hydroxylase could create an excess of dopamine.

Some medicines that are effective in the treatment of schizophrenia have strong effects on the noradrenaline system and relatively weaker effects on the dopamine system. Also, abnormally high levels of noradrenaline have been found in the brains of schizophrenic patients and in substances that contain neurochemicals derived from the brain (the cerebral spinal fluid and blood).

Greater promise seemed to be offered by research into the neurotransmitter, **5-hydroxytryptamine (5-HT** or **serotonin)**. This is related to, among other drugs, LSD and ecstasy (MDMA), and generally thought to be responsible for the communication of pleasure within the brain. Although much research has been conducted into possible links between a deficiency of 5-HT and schizo-phrenia—particularly in the 1950s—modern psychiatry is more interested in the long-term effects of 5-HT deple-tion, usually via MDMA abuse, on mood and depressive illness. This is not to suggest that 5-HT is not implicated in schizophrenia. Today's research, rather, focuses on the idea that an *excess* of the neurotransmitter may pre-cipitate, if not cause, the illness.

This hypothesis is backed up by the finding that a new neuroleptic drug called **Clozapine**, which we shall discuss later, is known to affect both the 5-HT and dopamine systems in the brain; its beneficial action may be due to a capacity to balance the activity of these two chemicals.

Brain abnormalities and the genetics of schizophrenia

As we have noted, there is no one-to-one correspondence between any one of these abnormalities and schizophrenia. Indeed, the sheer number of exceptions to the rule may cast doubt on the case for any necessary correlation between the two.

We should not, however, forget the possibility that all the abnormalities—genetic, structural, functional, biochemical, or otherwise may be causes in any individual case. This is to say that certain schizophrenics develop the illness for one of the reasons examined above, while others acquire it for quite other reasons. Each may be a 'cause' if we can attribute the signs and symptoms of schizophrenia to their presence.

Without having discovered an overall cause for schizophrenia, we have at least moved closer to identifying the areas and systems of the brain in which the abnormalities responsible for the illness are concentrated. Applying the knowledge we have acquired, we can now progress to asking the question, 'What causes neurotransmitter dysfunction?'

In the following passages we examine additional evidence suggesting that the genes that cause schizophrenia also cause brain dysfunction. These studies involve those who, although not schizophrenic themselves, are at high risk of carrying the gene because they are parents, siblings, or children of schizophrenic people.

Smooth pursuit eye movement dysfunction

This phenomenon, whereby the patient's eyes follow moving objects in jagged and jerky movements, rather than in a smooth sweep, tends to occur among schizophrenics even when they are 'well'. It is, therefore, a useful indicator of the illness. More significantly still, as well as occurring among some 70 per cent of sufferers, it is noted in around 45 per cent of their immediate relations.

The work of researchers, initiated by Dr Philip Holzman at Harvard University, during the past decade has led many to conclude that the gene responsible for eye movement dysfunction may also cause schizophrenia. As the reader will recall from our discussion of previous attempts to identify genes that may be close neighbours of the schizophrenic gene, this is an important breakthrough.

Attentional dysfunction

Attention deficits, which have been studied in relation to schizophrenia since the days of Kraepelin and Bleuler are important not only because of their usefulness in understanding the nature of schizophrenic brain disturbances, but also by dint of their relevance to genetic and biological factors. Several such disorders have been noted both in schizophrenics and in their healthy relatives. Measured with a task known as the continuous performance test or CPT, poor attention, like smooth pursuit eye movement dysfunction, emerges as a strong candidate for a biological characteristic of the schizophrenia gene. Certainly, the children of schizophrenic children perform poorly on the CPT, a fact that may prove predictive of schizophrenia in adolescence.

Schizophrenia: a neurodevelopmental brain disorder

The research we have so far considered suggests that schizophrenia occurs when abnormal genes lead to brain dysfunction. In some cases, an environmental agent may be needed to trigger this process.

The generic term for such illnesses is **neurodevelopmental disorders**. Expressed simply, the brain does not develop properly owing to design faults in the genetic blueprint according to which it is built. It may be that certain brain cells do not 'migrate' properly during development, that is to say they do not locate themselves in the right place to connect with one another in specific patterns; some cells may be in the wrong place; some do not make necessary connections, while others make connections which should not occur.

If the root cause of these problems is genetic, why should they lie dormant for so long in so many cases? The average age of onset is between 18 and 25 for men and 26 to 45 for women. If the fault lies with the genetic blueprint, ought we not to see evidence for it in the early developmental phase (i.e. childhood)?

The answer may, of course, be that problems *do* exist in schizophrenic children, but that they are far too subtle to detect. Dr Barbara Fish of the University of California at Los Angeles and Dr Joseph Marcus at the University of Chicago showed that the children of schizophrenic parents also measured noticeable neurological abnormalities when tested in childhood.

These studies indicate that the pre-schizophrenic brain is indeed abnormal, but do not explain why the onset of schizophrenia usually occurs in late adolescence or early adulthood. One likely explanation, however, is that the area of the brain most commonly implicated in schizophrenia, the frontal cortex, is one of the last areas of the brain to develop fully. When this and other brain areas cannot perform the functions necessary for people to cope with the transition from adolescence to adulthood, schizophrenia may ensue. Where patients first develop the illness long after the brain has completed its development, it may be due to the stress of environmental factors.

Conclusion

We have now examined the central questions that an illness such as schizophrenia pose to the scientific community. Let us briefly recap our findings.

We have discovered that approximately 1 per cent of the general population will suffer from this condition, and that individuals are most vulnerable at quite specific periods of their lives.

We have established that heredity almost certainly plays a role in the repetition of the illness through the generations, but the exact mechanism of transmission has yet to be discovered.

We can be equally confident in stating that adverse environmental factors that occur during fetal development play a role in causation of some cases of schizophrenia. Moreover, adverse circumstances appear to modify its course, affecting the patient's outlook for the worse. We have seen that concepts such as the *schizophrenogenic mother* and *schizophrenia as a symptom of a sick society* have thankfully given way to more rational theories that do not respectively apportion individual blame or demand wholesale social reconstruction in place of practical, sympathetic treatment.

We can be reasonably sure that schizophrenia is a brain disease of some sort, owing to the disproportionately high incidence of certain forms of brain dysfunction among sufferers. Many of these observable brain defects—such as enlarged ventricles—are not shared by all, or even by a majority of sufferers and we are currently unable to state exactly what sort of disease it might be.

We seem to have narrowed down a likely cause of schizophrenia in some patients to malfunctions within the brain's neurotransmitter systems, but far more evidence is required before we can say with certainty that such malfunctions can be considered the cause of the illness.

What, then, of our final question? *Can schizophrenia be prevented, alleviated, or cured?* These questions and the matters that arise from their consideration will form the basis for the remaining chapters in this book.

Section 3

Meeting the challenge of schizophrenia

10

Introduction

Canst thou not minister to a mind diseased,
Pluck from the memory a rooted sorrow,
Raze out the written troubles of the brain,
And with some sweet oblivious antidote
Cleanse the stuffed bosom of that perilous stuff
Which weighs upon the heart?

Shakespeare: *Macbeth*, V, iii, 42

A case study

Allan is a 47-year-old divorced, white male with an 18-year history of untreated schizophrenia. He presented as a grossly dishevelled individual with a bizarre appearance and behaviour. His head was shaven but for a thin strip of hair resembling a mohawk, over which he wore an aviator's hat with earflaps, over which he wore a bright yellow Italian cycling helmet. He was also wearing a long-sleeved thermal undershirt underneath a short-sleeved Lacoste shirt, through the collar of which he wore a necktie. His trousers were tucked into military boots and held up by a woman's-style leather belt three inches wide. His inappropriate laughter, which became uncontrollable at times, revealed extremely poor dental hygiene; many of his teeth were missing and those remaining were jagged and badly stained. He carried with him six plastic bags full of returnable cans and a cloth sack full of papers which he described as important research documents of the *Mission Institute*. This, Allan explained, is a 'one-man, international operation devoted to collecting information on topics of interest to me'. The title of one of his projects reads, *A*

Linear Study of the Lives of One Hundred Gifted Artists to Prove or Disprove a Statistical Correlation between Sibling Ordinality in the Nuclear Family Unit and Artistic 'Giftedness' in the Area of Sculpture Represented in 'Public Monuments'. The Institute is also said to be researching and developing an invention called a *Flexible Modular Containerization Compression System*, a machine designed to flatten cans to a thickness roughly that of a coin and sort them automatically.

The above titles represent good examples of Allan's verbal style, which tends to be highly intellectualized but lacking in content. Other informative speech samples come from his personal research into schizophrenia, a disorder he knows afflicts him: 'Functional schizophrenics perceive themselves through the eyes of others but fail to identify the process as such, which means that Sigmund Freud was 100 per cent correct in his analysis of Judge Daniel Schrader ... Functional schizophrenics insidiously mould themselves into schizophrenic pseudo-communities ... this is the same for schizophrenics all over the world, in France, Italy, Australia, Germany, the Island off Corsica, Nigeria, ... etc.'

At the age of 29, when the subject reported first experiencing psychotic symptoms, he had earned two masters degrees and was teaching part-time at the junior college level. In his own descriptive words, he found himself warding off hostile forces not experienced by others. He came to distrust contacts with other persons and institutions of all kinds. He became secretive, withdrawn, and sequestered, until finally his paranoia led him to make a suicide attempt by closing the kitchen doors and turning on the gas stove. His wife found him in a confused and psychotic state and brought him to a local mental institution where he was kept for three days and treated with Valium, Librium, and Thorazine (Largactyl). He stayed on these medications for three weeks and then refused to take them. He has not been hospitalized or medicated since. He claims that since the onset of his psychosis he has gradually developed an individual lifestyle, free from the constraints of institutions, with which he is quite satisfied.

Allan denies experiencing auditory or visual hallucinations, although he does report a possible somatic hallucination, a 'tightness of the brain' which, despite his numerous visits to doctors, remains medically unexplained. There is no evidence of any major affective disturbance or of any substance abuse; the subject credibly states that he is opposed to drugs of all kinds.

Clinician's diagnosis and comments

Allan was diagnosed as suffering from chronic schizophrenia, with particularly pronounced paranoid ideation. Positive symptoms of the illness were manifested in his extremely dishevelled appearance and behaviour, thought disorder, and delusions of paranoia and grandiosity. Negative symptoms noted included self-neglect and poor personal hygiene, and poor eye-contact. Despite his non-compliance with his medication regime, he has managed to avoid psychiatric treatment for a long time without severe consequences. He also gains a measure of emotional satisfaction in pursuing his strange interests.

Allan's story, and that of many schizophrenics, is a tragic tale of unfulfilled potential and downward social drift. A clever, highly educated, and articulate man in early middle-age would normally be approaching his peak years in terms of earnings, job satisfaction, and enjoyment of family life. Instead, we meet a bizarre character who has not worked for 18 years, save for the frankly crackpot writings that compose his 'one-man research project'. His wife has divorced him since the onset of his illness. He refuses further psychiatric treatment and medication. In all, there seems little chance of his ever contributing to a community in which he feels comfortable and secure.

What can we do for people like Allan?

Using the words with which we framed our final *central question* in Section Two, we can state that although schizophrenia cannot be cured, it *can* be treated and its symptoms alleviated. In this section we examine the treatment of schizophrenia by modern psychiatry; in the final section we shall suggest and assess ways in which those with the illness and those involved with them can learn to cope with its many demands and challenges.

Prevention

First, however, we will deal quickly with the issue of *preventing* schizophrenia. Advances in modern genetics have enabled scientists to identify the genes responsible for certain serious illnesses, and so predict the probability of them being passed to subsequent generations.

We have already seen that despite the wealth of research material linking schizophrenia to heredity, researchers have yet to identify the gene or genes responsible for its transmission. Furthermore, we can only make rough predictions regarding whether the children of a given future generation will inherit the condition. Finally, and perhaps most crucially, schizophrenia seems to require some environmental *trigger* in some, if not every person who will develop it.

Because we cannot predict schizophrenia it cannot now be prevented by addressing its genetic underpinnings or by manipulating the postnatal environment. Yet the prevention of schizophrenia is an achievable scientific goal. What is needed to make this a reality? More research to identify predictors of schizophrenia onset and the development of drugs that target the signs of an emerging disorder.

Can schizophrenia be cured?

Cold logic suggests that without a definite understanding of the *cause* of an illness, we cannot hope to cure it. Strangely enough, this is not strictly the case in medical science. Indeed, sometimes the exact cause of some conditions (eg depression) continues to elude researchers long after simple and effective treatments have been discovered and employed. Schizophrenia, sadly, is not among this number. Not only is the cause of the illness unknown, but we currently possess only the vaguest idea of what form of treatment might ultimately provide a cure.

This does not mean that people do not *get better* from schizophrenia with the help of medical science. It is simply that there can be no absolute guarantee that they will not suffer a relapse. Our response to the illness at present is primarily research-based. In the short term, we need to develop more effective and trouble-free treatments for the illness's symptoms; in the medium term, we need better to understand the mechanism by which it is transmitted down the generations; in the long term, we hope to find a cure. There is, naturally, no guarantee that this will be forthcoming. Some diseases are still classified as *incurable*, a frank admission that we cannot at present conceive of the kind of medical advance that would be required before they could be eradicated. Schizophrenia does not officially stand in this category, but it would be a brave researcher who would state with confidence that the condition is definitely curable.

Alleviation

The final of our central questions, *can schizophrenia be alleviated?* brings us into more optimistic territory, for the answer is emphatically positive. In the following chapter, we examine the main forms of treatment available to the sufferer.

11

Treating schizophrenia

There is a pleasure sure
In being mad which none but madmen know.

John Dryden: *The Spanish friar*. 1681

Treatment through the ages

We have doubtless all heard at least someone voice the
opinion that 'madmen are the happiest people on the
face of the earth'. It 'stands to reason', he or she will tell
you: 'the mentally ill inhabit a world of their own' free
from the concerns of ordinary adults; they giggle and
laugh uncontrollably; they daydream happily, while the
rest of us go about our drab, demanding, 'sane' lives.

By now even a reader with no previous knowledge of
schizophrenia should be sufficiently well acquainted with
the facts of the illness to refute this facile and thoughtless
nonsense without our help. Sadly, however, one encounters similar views all too frequently among otherwise
intelligent people.

In many ancient civilizations, and in some developing
countries today, schizophrenia has been seen to betoken
sorcery, demonic possession, or, in complete contrast, a
state of especial spiritual sanctity. Thousands of mentally
ill people have been forced to confess to witchcraft, or
have been exorcized, often by authorities whose over-
zealous methods have resulted in the mutilation or death
of their charges. Conversely, in other cultures the

schizophrenic has been worshipped, or at least protected by his community, which credited him with religious powers and considered his presence among them a divine blessing.

Although the wilder superstitions surrounding schizophrenia and similar illnesses died out, in the Western world at least, with the evolution of medicine it is reasonable to say that no attempt was made to *treat* schizophrenia until well into the latter half of the nineteenth century. (In saying *schizophrenia* we are not forgetting that pre-Bleuler the illness had no such name.) 'Madness' of every type was often lumped together, and 'lunatics' subjected to the same regime of enforced confinement in so-called 'asylums'. The most notorious, such as London's Bedlam, were little more than human zoos, where the sick were often chained up in wretched conditions, and their families left to provide them with adequate food and clothing. Perhaps most shameful was the practice of conducting paid tours of these miserable institutions for those whose thirst for novelty tended towards morbid curiosity.

As medicine and the young science of psychiatry grew in sophistication and influence, so the lunatic asylum in time gave way to the *mental hospital*, an institution dedicated to the care and treatment of its patients, but still with an emphasis on confinement away from society proper. Often situated in rural areas or the outskirts of cities, and serving vast catchment areas, the typical mental hospital was essentially an in-patient institution, caring for the mentally ill for much of their natural lives.

Although many of these hospitals remain standing to this day, their function in the United Kingdom and the United States, has changed dramatically to encompass a shift towards more flexible systems of treatment. We shall examine and evaluate the success of these new systems in the appropriate place; in the meantime, let us return to what happens today when a schizophrenic person seeks treatment for the first time.

What brings patients to treatment?

As can be imagined from the various case studies we have reproduced, the onset of schizophrenia can be a frightening occurrence for both the patient himself and his family. In some cases, the treatment process may be precipitated by some crisis in the patient's life, which may have driven the sufferer to some form of bizarre behaviour.

In other cases, a steady accretion of symptoms occurs. This no less harrowing for patients and their families. The illness may first be manifested by the expression of the odd belief that friends, relatives, or even celebrities are trying to harm them; that others can hear their thoughts as if spoken aloud; that voices talk to them, even when they are alone. In addition, they cannot express feelings and thoughts clearly and are frustrated by the disbelief of family and friends. They can see that something is wrong, but do not consider themselves as requiring medical help. Well-meaning relatives may try to reason with them, but such discussions often deteriorate into heated arguments.

Relatives struggle to cope with bizarre beliefs typical of schizophrenia. To the patient, these beliefs are *real* and not the effects of a brain disease or mental illness. Some seek treatment on their own, but for extraordinary reasons. A patient may appear at an emergency room requesting the doctors there to remove a radio transmitter from his brain. In one recorded case, someone sought help with computer chips placed in her teeth by the CIA. Yet another believed that rats were eating his intestines.

The patient's arrival at the doctor's office, for whatever reason, is no guarantee that he or she will be treated. Many react very negatively to the suggestion of a psychiatric examination and may leave the office in high indignation. Friends, relatives, and the doctor himself may be seen as persecutors in their delusional systems.

Treatment begins with diagnosis

We have already examined, in some detail, the methods of diagnosis commonly applied by psychiatrists. Several additional points need to be made at this stage. In the foregoing paragraphs, we are assuming the place of consultation to be a psychiatric institution and the doctor a qualified psychiatrist.

First, there are cases in which patients present to the doctor in an extremely disturbed state in which a reliable diagnosis cannot be made. In such circumstances, the doctor may need first to calm the patient—usually by use of an antipsychotic medicine—before the diagnostic process can commence.

It should also be stressed, to families in particular, that a comprehensive diagnosis may take a considerable time to achieve; the doctor will require many medical tests: X-rays, blood tests, and other physical examinations. These are needed to be sure that the apparent symptoms of schizophrenia are not due to a physical illness. It would be tragic if the doctor did not learn that street drugs, a brain tumour, or some other problem had caused the symptoms observed. Laboratory tests will be required to eliminate these possibilities, and these take time. Families should be aware that doctors are as anxious as they to reach answers to these questions and do their best to conquer the inescapable sense of impatience they will experience.

We shall look at the make-up of a typical health team that may treat a patient a little later, but now is the time to clear up one potential source of confusion among families and patients alike. Some health systems employ a psychiatrist and a psychologist alongside each other to work with the patient. What, people often wonder, is the difference? In brief, it is this: the psychiatrist is a physician whose training allows him to prescribe drugs and to monitor their effects on patients. Psychologists are not physicians, and cannot prescribe. They are, however, trained to assess psychopathology (i.e. defects in mental function and its effects upon thinking and emotion). They are specially trained to treat schizophrenia using psychological and behavioural techniques.

The first form of treatment of schizophrenia we shall consider is the use of specialist medications. The use of these drugs is in almost every sense *the primary issue* affecting the treatment of this disease today. It is viewed by most psychiatrists as offering the best hope of real progress in alleviating the condition. At the same time, the very drugs which can do so much to heal, have themselves been implicated in the deterioration of some of those they were designed to help.

12
Biological therapies

Neuroleptic drugs

By far the most widely used group of drugs in treating schizophrenia are the **neuroleptics**. Their ability to alleviate the symptoms of schizophrenia in some people makes them likely to be the drug of first choice when patients have active schizophrenic symptoms, such as delusions or hallucinations. At this stage the patients are so completely out of touch with reality that they cannot correctly perceive efforts to help them. Neuroleptics seem able to break down the barriers of emotion and communication disturbance that separate patients from their friends, family, and therapists, thereby easing the path to effective treatment.

Neuroleptic drugs, also known as **antipsychotics**, were introduced in the 1950s. Since then, world-wide studies have testified to their effectiveness in treating schizophrenic symptoms, with an average of two-thirds of patients showing a significant improvement.

International variations in the brand names of these drugs make it impossible for us to provide a full list of them here. If you require detailed information about the type of drug prescribed and its particular effects, your doctor will answer your questions or be equipped with the reference literature needed to deal with your enquiries.

The sheer number of neuroleptic drugs, and the different effects they can produce in individual patients, means that the doctor cannot hope always to find exactly the right drug for the patient at the first attempt. Again, patients' families may require forebearance. The doctor may also need to prescribe other drugs simultaneously to deal with medical problems, but it is highly unlikely that he would prescribe a *cocktail* of more than one neuroleptic drug.

Different neuroleptics are frequently used to manage symptoms of the illness at different stages of its course. It is also possible that a patient does not respond well to one type of drug, in which case the doctor may have to switch to another. Whatever the reason, one should not be alarmed if several drug regimes are tried before the optimum one is discovered. This practice is common and should not be interpreted as the doctor 'trying anything and everything' in the hope of hitting on an effective treatment.

Neuroleptic side-effects

Unfortunately, neuroleptic drugs bring with them the risk of side-effects. These range from the mildly unpleasant to the debilitating, and in very rare circumstances, death has been known to occur. Many of these problems can, however, be avoided or controlled so long as the patient remains in the care of a psychiatrist.

The most common side-effects of these drugs are categorized as **extrapyramidal**. These affect the neural system in the brain that helps to control movement. There are three basic types of extrapyramidal side-effects, known as **dystonia, akathisia**, and **pseudo-parkinsonism**, and they occur in 40 to 60 per cent of patients.

Dystonia is the name given to involuntary muscle contractions, typically affecting the head and face. They make the patient feel stiff, and may be uncomfortable or even painful. Facial appearance and body posture may be distorted, which can make the sufferer embarrassed in social situations.

Akathisia is a subjective feeling of restlessness. It may be expressed physically by pacing, rocking from foot to foot, other motor activity, or insomnia. Again, the symptoms can range from the mildly irritating to the extremely uncomfortable.

Pseudo-parkinsonism, as its name suggests, is a condition virtually indistinguishable from the neurological illness, Parkinson's disease. It includes tremors, stiffness, and sometimes lack of movement. The patient's face may show little expressiveness, almost as if a mask were being worn.

Perhaps the most common, if not the most severe problem with all these side-effects is that they tend to discourage the patient from taking the prescribed medication, and provide a reasonable explanation for his reluctance to do so.

The extrapyramidal side-effects usually occur within a few days of treatment, and may be sufficiently severe to require medical advice quickly. Doctors are usually able to minimize these problems, often by switching to a different neuroleptic drug. Another possibility is to treat the patient with drugs specially designed to control the side-effects.

If neuroleptics are used over a long period, there is the possibility that a neurological complication known as **tardive dyskinesia** may develop. Like the extrapyramidal symptoms, this condition produces uncontrollable muscle movements, usually of the face. Sufferers repeatedly smack their lips together, stick out their tongue, grimace, and move their chin from side to side. Withdrawal from neuroleptics may stop these *dyskinetic* symptoms, but the syndrome can continue, sometimes permanently, even after their discontinuation.

Research suggests that approximately 20 per cent of patients treated with neuroleptics will develop tardive dyskinesia. There is at this stage, however, no way of knowing prior to the commencement of treatment, who these patients will be. For this reason alone, neuroleptic treatment must be overseen by a psychiatrist or other doctor experienced and skilled in its use, and careful, regular observation of the patient conducted to ensure that any early signs of the condition are noticed while they are easiest to treat.

Neuroleptic malignant syndrome is a severe side-effect of treatment with neuroleptic drugs. The clinical signs of the syndrome are fever, a rapid heartbeat, muscle stiffness, altered consciousness, abnormal blood pressure, shortness of breath, and sweating. If a psychiatrist suspects neuroleptic malignant syndrome, a blood test will be taken. Abnormal levels of specific constituents of blood are common indicators of the syndrome. This is one case in which the neuroleptic drug used will be immediately discontinued, thereby reversing a process that would otherwise lead swiftly to death. The reader will be relieved to hear that neuroleptic malignant syndrome is extremely rare.

Low-dose neuroleptic treatment

As soon as it became apparent that neuroleptic side-effects were common, and that some were severe, clinical scientists sought to develop new dosing strategies. Their goal was to give patients the smallest amount of the drug that would have a therapeutic effect. The cornerstone of this new treatment regime was that patients should take no more of a drug than was medically essential.

These scientists quickly learned that excessive use of neuroleptics is most likely to occur when the dose originally prescribed to combat extremely distressing symptoms is not reduced once these symptoms have abated. The highly agitated and disturbed schizophrenic requires drugs in dosages that are excessive after the florid stage of the illness has passed. The seriousness of neuroleptic side-effects prohibits the extended use of large doses unless the efficacy of the drug will be diminished when administered in smaller doses.

Ideally, drug treatment should be reduced soon after the initial symptoms are relieved. If patients continue to receive this lower dose after leaving the hospital, this is known as *maintenance* treatment, since it literally helps to maintain the patient in the community. Although the effectiveness of maintenance therapy has been amply demonstrated in general, it cannot guarantee that severe symptoms will not return. Schizophrenia is classed as a *relapsing illness*—that is, a condition where relapse is an ever-present, if not an inevitable possibility—and it is estimated that around half the schizophrenics on drug maintenance will suffer some relapse within two years. These are sobering statistics, yet two points do offer reassurance: first, the relapse may be by no means as severe as the initial onset of the illness; second, one should bear in mind that those *not* treated suffer an 84 per cent rate of relapse.

An alternative to low-dose treatment is *intermittent* treatment, in which the patient is medicated only when symptoms return and is completely drug-free while in remission. This strategy does have clear advantages but requires almost constant observation by family and clinicians so that early signs of pending relapse can be swiftly dealt with.

Depot injections

Some neuroleptic drugs can be administered as depot injections. Under this system, the patient attends his local mental health clinic on a regular, say fortnightly, basis to receive an intramuscular injection of the neuroleptic of choice.

Clozapine and the 'new breed' of neuroleptic drugs

Academic and drug company scientists around the world are constantly trying to create more effective drugs for the treatment of schizophrenia.

Much attention has been focused on a new generation of neuroleptics, the first of which, Clozapine, has now been available for several years. This drug, aside from benefiting some patients who do not respond to other neuroleptics, produces far less pronounced extrapyramidal side-effects and is less likely to cause tardive dyskinesia, possibly even suppressing the syndrome when it is caused by other neuroleptics. There is, however, a risk attached to Clozapine: in a small proportion of users it causes a condition known as **agranulocytosis** which renders the body incapable of making the normal number of white blood cells. This in turn renders the body unable to fight infection, a life-threatening condition. Approximately 2 per cent of Clozapine users will develop agranulocytosis after a year of treatment with the drug. Precisely which patients these will be can only be determined by regular blood tests weekly for the first eighteen weeks of treatment and fortnightly thereafter. Owing to its potentially fatal side-effect and the difficulty presented in monitoring those receiving it, Clozapine is often the drug of last resort.

The advent of Clozapine was, nonetheless, an exciting event in the development of psychiatric medications, since it heralded a new direction in research and provided symptom relief to many patients who fared poorly on other medicines. What if a drug or drugs could be found that offered Clozapine's numerous benefits, but did not cause agranulocytosis?

Risperidone, a drug that blocks both the dopamine and 5-HT receptors appears equally effective in controlling positive and negative symptoms of schizophrenia, a characteristic that has thus far eluded almost all of the most commonly prescribed neuroleptic drugs. Equally encouragingly, it does not cause agranulocytosis, but seems to share Clozapine's propensity to cause few, if any, extrapyramidal symptoms in the average patient.

One must, however, temper the kind of heady optimism that often greets the development of *wonder drugs* with a word of caution. Although Clozapine and Risperidone are landmarks in the treatment of schizophrenia, there is no guarantee that they will suit everybody's needs. Fortunately, new drugs are currently being developed. Two new drugs, olanzapine and sertindole, are likely to further help many schizophrenia patients.

The development of these new generation neuroleptics is a genuinely exciting phenomenon. When, as is the case with schizophrenia, an illness proves so resistant to research and treatment, such advances should be encouraged and celebrated.

Other biological treatments

Numerous other types of drug have been suggested for the treatment of schizophrenia. It is beyond the scope of this book to discuss them more than fleetingly here, but families should be aware that although the drug of first choice is likely to be a neuroleptic, other medicines may be used as an adjunct to it or, in special cases, alone in their own right.

Examples of these drugs include **lithium**, which has been shown to be effective in some cases, particularly when prescribed in conjunction with a neuroleptic. Benzodiazapines, such as **diazepam (Valium)** or **chlordiazepoxide (Librium)**, normally prescribed for anxiety, help some patients.

Anticonvulsants, which prevent convulsive fits in epileptics, sometimes work for schizophrenics, especially those with abnormal brain waves as measured by an electro encephalogram (EEG). They do not, however, appear to be effective as a maintenance treatment.

Electroconvulsive therapy (ECT), known in the popular press as *shock treatment* because it involves the application of an electric impulse to the brain, is perhaps one of medicine's most controversial and misunderstood forms of treatment. Anyone familiar with Ken Kesey's *One flew over the cuckoo's nest*, or similar fictional portrayals of old-style mental institutions, is likely to view ECT as it is often known, as a pseudo-treatment intended to render troublesome patients docile and more readily controllable. In terms of its public image, ECT has been so generally vilified that rational evaluations of its actual therapeutic value are hardly thought worth publicizing.

The truth is that ECT can be of real benefit to some people with severe depression. It has been tried on schizophrenic patients, but has not proved useful and only in extremely rare circumstances might this form of treatment be suggested.

Compliance with medical treatment

If so many patients dislike their effects and decide not to take medicines, why should they be persuaded, cajoled, and in some cases forced to do so against their expressed will? Is not the psychiatrist ignoring the wishes of his patient, and generally behaving in a presumptuous and patronizing manner?

It is certainly true that many people with schizophrenia do not want to take their medication. Some 50 per cent of patients in the community neglect or refuse their medication, and even among those in hospital the figure is as high as 20 per cent.

This may be owing to **paranoid ideation** (the suspicion that the drug is a poison or truth drug of some sort), or to an unpleasant reaction to the first drug prescribed. Since the schizophrenic patient is often unable to weigh the advantages and disadvantages of adhering to a medication regime, this latter consideration may decide the matter.

There is also the problem that a patient living a chaotic lifestyle may forget or neglect to take even a drug to which he has no rooted objection. Hence, nearly half of all patients being treated for schizophrenia do not take their medication after leaving hospital. This figure includes those receiving depot injections, who fail to turn up at the clinic at the prescribed time or at all.

Criticism of biological treatments

The neuroleptics themselves have been criticized vociferously by the families of some schizophrenics, certain psychiatrists, and even nationally influential charities whose perceived authority and expertize in the field of mental illness lends additional weight to their views.

The claims of what we might term the *anti-drug lobby* are not simply mischievous and they are not wholly without foundation. Since the authors of this book believe strongly in the value of antipsychotic drugs, it is, we feel, incumbent upon us to present our own responses to the most commonly voiced of these views. The reader will almost certainly encounter them, and should be aware of the evidence usually cited by proponents of both sides of the argument.

Are neuroleptics chemical strait-jackets?

According to those who express this view, neuroleptic drugs are used by psychiatrists to pacify schizophrenic patients, strip them of their creativity and individuality, and render them incapable of controlling their own destiny. In brief, the psychiatrist exercises a form of mind control, making the patient more readily *processed* by the prevailing mental health system, while covering up his own inability to cure or alleviate the symptoms afflicting the patient.

We have already seen that some social theorists believe that the psychiatrist is a modern day mountebank, a kind of snake oil selling charlatan, who legitimates the sufferings of a sick society by giving pseudo-scientific names to the natural symptoms of daily life in a sick and sick-making society. This is, however, an extreme view, the main gist of which we have already addressed.

The position adopted by more temperate critics of neuroleptic drugs is that their negative side-effects greatly outweigh their benefits for the patient. Is there substance to this claim?

As is true of any powerful drug that affects the brain and central nervous system, a neuroleptic may for a time give rise to quite pronounced and debilitating side-effects.

Some of these, it must be admitted, may persist throughout treatment with varying degrees of severity. Moreover, tardive dyskinesia is sometimes irreversible and other rare conditions (neuroleptic malignant syndrome, agranulocytosis), can be fatal. Many of the side-effects most prevalent in the early phase of the drug's prescription—trembling, slowness of movement and thought, tics, and compulsive movements; and development of a *moon-faced* appearance—usually pass away. The patient will then begin to regain something of his former demeanour and appearance. The disinterested observer, however, seeing the patient at the height of his initial reaction to the new drug, might well conclude that the patient was, in his more lucid moments at least, far happier, healthier, and more generally *alive* than under this dreadful new medication.

The third, and perhaps most forceful argument against the widespread prescribing of neuroleptic drugs involves references to trends in mental health care in the United Kingdom and United States, and may have limited relevance for readers outside those countries. We include it, first, because it is of real importance to people in these countries, and second, because the trends we refer to are likely to become more widespread geographically in the coming years.

According to this third view, the use of neuroleptics is at least in part *politically* motivated. There has been a progressive shift in mental health-care policy under recent UK and US governments away from long-stay in-patient care in large hospitals towards a system where hospital admissions are kept to a minimum, with the emphasis on brief in-patient assessment and treatment, followed by ongoing out-patient *care in the community*.

The primary complaint of those who object to neuroleptic medication on these grounds is not that it does away with the need for hundreds of long-stay mental hospitals dotted around a country. Many campaigning mental health organizations and charities perform an extremely valuable service in providing ground-level help for schizophrenics returning to society proper. What rightly concerns this particular group, but is far less temperately expressed by other, more radical factions, is the fear that neuroleptics effectively *institutionalize* the patient *in society*, creating what amounts in William Blake's evocative phrase to 'mind-forged manacles'.

It is certainly true that a schizophrenic regularly taking an appropriate neuroleptic is less troublesome to society than another who refuses his medication. The reason, however, is quite simply that the former is more likely to be free of positive symptoms. He is not *doped*; he is well. Again we emphasize that these drugs cannot always prevent relapse, and that they do not work for everyone. Be this as it may, it remains fundamentally wrong to ascribe to psychiatrists the ruthless desire to *control* their patients, whether for reasons of political compliance or personal convenience. Although psychiatry has, at times, been used for political purposes, these abuses were reflections of the nature of the government in question, and not of the practice of psychiatric medicine.

As regards the move away from generalized long-term in-patient care, the vast majority of psychiatrists share the belief that the correct place for any person is within the community. This principle is naturally subject to the proviso that they *can cope with life therein and present no danger to themselves or others*. The needs of the individual patient are paramount; a clinician who excluded neuroleptic drugs from his range of treatments could not hope properly to address those needs.

13
Non-biological therapies

Not all treatments for schizophrenia involve the use of drugs. **Psychological treatment** is a broad term used to describe any therapeutic approach seeking to modify thoughts and behaviour without medicine. They are not necessarily an alternative to drug therapies; the two may be used in conjunction. Indeed, this seems to be the ideal treatment plan for many schizophrenic patients.

We should remind the reader here that not all psychiatrists agree with each other over many issues relating to schizophrenia. This fact should not, and in the vast majority *will* not affect the general method or standard of care you or your relatives receive. Like all professionals, psychiatrists learn early in their career that their own opinions and theories concerning an illness and its treatment, must only decide their exact regime of treatment within universally agreed limits. These limits may take the form of guidelines or absolute rules, according to a number of factors. The system is regulated by professional associations, specialist organizations, and ultimately, the law. This is an important point for relations of schizophrenics to keep in mind.

Psychotherapy

This involves the patient meeting regularly with a therapist to talk about his problems and concerns in general. These may or may not be directly related to the patient's schizophrenia and its causes. There are many types of psychotherapy which may differ dramatically. Some involve the patient recalling events from childhood, with the therapist saying very little but trying to guide the patient towards insights into his life and problems; others deal only with the patient's specific day-to-day problems, such as finding a job.

How valuable is psychotherapy in the treatment of schizophrenia? **The American Psychiatric Association Commission on Psychotherapies** conducted a major study of this subject and concluded that, although useful for many other psychiatric disorders, psychotherapy was not an effective treatment for schizophrenia. Without ruling out its use altogether, it was deemed suitable only as an adjunct to, and not a replacement for, drug treatment.

In its correct context, then, the psychotherapist's skills have considerable value. The development of a productive patient–therapist relationship can help foster compliance with a drug therapy regime and help the patient to deal with the social and psychological consequences of the illness. As such, psychotherapy can be a valuable ally of conventional drug therapy.

Behavioural therapy

Unlike other psychological treatments, behavioural therapy seeks exclusively to change the behaviour of schizophrenics—literally to alter what they do. The methods employed are governed by scientific principles of learning discovered by psychologists and supported by decades of research. Behavioural therapists view these principles as *scientific laws*, and believe that by their manipulation they can change behaviour in their patients.

The primary focus for such therapy is the schizophrenic's ability to deal with social situations. We know that schizophrenics have acute problems in this area and that many seek social isolation. We also know that over-stimulation of their social interactions can increase psychotic symptoms. There is, therefore a delicate balance to be found by counsellors and relatives, and the rehabilitation programme must be fully tailored to the needs of the individual patient. There are many alternatives available. In what follows, we briefly review three behavioural methods that have been used with success in the treatment of schizophrenia: *reward and punishment*, *social skills training*, and *family therapy*.

Reward and punishment

The title of this form of therapy almost renders explanations of it redundant. Used as an in-patient treatment, it seeks to modify the patient's behaviour by means of a *token economy* in which he receives small tokens for correct behaviour. These might take the form of poker chips, exchangeable for special foods, access to TV, and so on. Negative behaviour will result in their not being awarded. This therapy takes as its intellectual base the behaviourist philosophy of B.F. Skinner who believed that positive and negative *reinforcement* (i.e. reward and punishment) could modify human behaviour as effectively as that of rats. Without entirely denying its existence, the *inner life* as such held no interest whatsoever for Skinner. Schizophrenics, as we have seen, show every sign of having a rich, albeit disordered, inner life but may be incapable of expressing, much less controlling their social needs.

The primary difficulty with this type of therapy is that it may prove difficult for the patient to carry over into everyday life. Also, if the goal is to increase the frequency of a desired behaviour, the patient must be capable or willing to behave in an acceptable way *at least sometimes*, or there will be no opportunity to reward him, and so set the therapeutic process in motion. This is particularly the case in social behaviour where many schizophrenic patients are so completely withdrawn that, for practical purposes, they emit little if any appropriate behaviour.

To deal with this problem, therapists created response acquisition procedures to help sufferers develop responses to social stimuli. Since this work has mostly focused on social behaviour, these techniques are often referred to as social skills training.

Social skills training

This form of training is usually performed with groups of patients, in order to create an artificial social situation in which to teach social behaviour. Although the details of the method vary among hospitals and clinicians, each shares a common feature: the therapists actively teach the patients how to use verbal and non-verbal behaviour in social situations.

A typical programme might involve a group of three to four patients and two co-therapists. It will require the completion of a number of tasks which involve the patients in observing, analysing, and finally rehearsing forms of social behaviour.

In this particular example of a programme, the therapists begin by reviewing the progress made in the preceding session, with an emphasis on whether the patient managed to practice the behaviour in question *outside* the training environment. Next, a summary of the issues to be dealt with in the coming session is presented to clarify the usefulness of the behaviour in question in social situations. Since patients learn best by observation, the therapists next perform a role play of the skill to be learned or use a suitable video to exemplify the point.

Schizophrenic patients are often extremely withdrawn. They may also have very short attention spans. In order to stimulate discussion about the content of the session, the therapist may have to quiz the patients on what they have seen. Next, small groups of patients themselves practice the newly learned social behaviour in succession so that their performance can be videotaped for subsequent discussion by the group. This open discussion provides all patients with the opportunity to give and receive feedback, and to help each other to learn new skills. After the feedback discussion, the patients again work in pairs to master the skill by repeated practice. The session ends with the therapist asking the patients to practice the newly learned social skill *outside* the therapy session. Patients are usually set very reasonable goals; they might, for example, be asked to practice one of the skills they have learned once a day.

Family therapy

In an earlier chapter we noted that although the family environment does not play a role in the *aetiology* or cause of schizophrenia, it may affect the *course* of the illness. In practical terms, this means that certain types of family interaction may worsen schizophrenic symptoms and result in increased rates of relapse and hospitalization. Conversely, the right kind of behaviour by family and friends may reduce stress in the patient's life and maximize his chances of a favourable prognosis.

As pioneered by Dr Ian Falloon in the UK, there are three major components to behavioural family therapy: *education*, *communication*, and *problem-solving*.

The educational component tries to reduce any sense of self-blame among family members for their relative's illness. We have already seen how the impact of such emotions can only be negative for all concerned. In addition to learning about the biological basis of the illness, families are disabused of the notion of neuroleptics as *chemical strait-jackets*, and other similar misconceptions.

An apparently obvious but often essential lesson for parents to learn is that the schizophrenic cannot control his symptoms. Urging the patient to 'stop being paranoid' or criticizing his apathy and withdrawal will only create further stress and erect new barriers to effective treatment.

Relatives are also taught not to communicate high social or occupational expectations to the patient. This can be extremely difficult in situations where a formerly bright, or even brilliant child becomes unable to hold on to an undemanding low-paid job, or even to work at all. Nonetheless, the fact must be faced that many sufferers will never work and never marry. The goal of communication therapy is to help the family to understand what the patient is and is not capable of, and to assess honestly what constitutes realistic expectations in life.

Perhaps most importantly, families are taught to identify potential stresses for the patient in their home environment. This is no easy matter, as what constitutes *stress* will differ greatly from patient to patient. Moreover, the causes of stress may be hidden or buried by families— forms of marital rift, for example—so that they become too sensitive for the family to discuss openly. The therapist may need to assist the family to communicate concerning their own sources of stress before the matter of how these might be communicated to the schizophrenic family member can be broached.

Can these treatments work alone?

Although we have presented these psychological therapies in isolation both to one another and to drug therapies, have any of them alone proved effective in the management of schizophrenia? Put succinctly, the answer is *no*. This is not to say that a campaigning pressure group, for example, cannot ever produce a schizophrenic who, after declining all medication, *found sanity and stability* by use of, say, psychotherapy alone. Somewhere, doubtless, there is someone making the same claim for Zen yoga or aromatherapy. Without pouring scorn on these claims, the general experience of those involved with the treatment of schizophrenia is that the treatments outlined above are best employed as adjuncts to, rather than replacements for, treatment with neuroleptic medications.

This conclusion is almost universally agreed by psychiatrists and psychologists. It should, however, be noted that although therapy alone reduces the relapse rates of patients who have already been rehabilitated into the community, this improvement loses its effect after a year, except for those still receiving neuroleptic drugs. Maximum benefit, it seems, can be obtained from a combined regime of medication and behaviour therapy lasting for at least one year after the patient is discharged into the community.

Balanced against this must be the research finding that therapy had actually *hastened relapse* in some patients with severe schizophrenic symptoms. Many investigators have confirmed that too vigorous rehabilitation can result in over-stimulation and relapse of positive schizophrenic symptoms, such as delusions and hallucinations. For example, Dr J.K. Wing and his colleagues of the British Medical Research Council Social Psychiatry Research Unit reported in 1964 that delusions and hallucinations re-emerged in a group of chronic schizophrenic patients who were put directly into an industrial rehabilitation unit. This could have been prevented by adequate preparation of the patients, for example, by encouraging them to participate in the work periods on the ward, followed by sessions in the occupational training unit of the hospital.

Other types of therapy, if not performed carefully, may over-stimulate the patient and result in the reappearance of positive schizophrenic symptoms. For instance, intense group psychotherapy designed to uncover 'unconscious motivation' and 'role function' may worsen schizophrenic symptoms. Recreational therapy, occupational therapy, group activity, or resocializational therapy may also be potential sources of over-stimulation, if carried out too vigorously.

On the other hand, other studies have found a connection between an under-stimulating environment, such as the chronic wards of a large mental hospital, and negative schizophrenic symptoms—apathy, lack of initiative, slowness, social isolation, and poverty of speech. Therefore, in treating schizophrenics one walks a tightrope: under-stimulation may lead to negative symptoms on the one hand, and over-stimulation may lead to positive symptoms on the other. Neuroleptics can provide some protection against over-stimulation, but indiscriminate use of the drugs over a long period of time may lead to troublesome neurological complications in some patients. Behavioural therapies may encourage chronic patients to come out from their isolation, but can precipitate the reappearance of positive symptoms. In treating schizophrenic patients one is essentially aiming to provide the optimum conditions for extremely vulnerable people.

There will, however, necessarily be some people whom none of these treatments seem to benefit. What becomes of them? Such patients may require a considerable stay in a specialist hospital. In the following pages, we look at the modern psychiatric hospital, not only as a long-stay institute for the chronically ill patient, but as the backbone of today's mental health-care system.

The role of the hospital in modern mental health care

We have already stated that hospitals are rarely used for chronic care as in the past. Today, hospitalization is used for four basic reasons: *diagnostic evaluation*; *regulation of medication*; *reduction of danger to the patient or other*; and *acute management problems*. None of these functions can be discussed in isolation; several of these processes overlap, and each plays a part in the patient's experience of hospitalization. We shall therefore adopt a *patient-focused* approach to the issue of hospitalization.

In the remainder of this section we look at the circumstances under which most schizophrenics come into contact with the typical mental hospital, and examine the general treatment regime currently in practice within it.

In the final part of the book we shall offer a short evaluation of the medical and political philosophies that have created this system. We shall discuss the quality of service it offers the schizophrenic in terms of his personal development and assess the general *prognosis* (medical outlook) for schizophrenia generally. Finally, we shall look briefly at various coping strategies available to sufferers and their carers.

Contact with the hospital

Any schizophrenic patient who is receiving treatment for his condition will at some point visit a mental hospital.

Normally, this will occur as the result of a referral from the patient's family doctor, and the purpose will be to obtain a professional diagnosis from a psychiatric specialist.

In some rare cases, the patient may simply seek out the hospital for himself, complaining of schizophrenic symptoms (usually positive) and requesting to see a doctor. Such cases are uncommon, primarily because people experiencing delusions or hallucinations are unlikely to identify the nature of their problems and act logically to alleviate them. This is not to suggest that schizophrenics do not turn up at mental hospitals demanding treatment; those who do, however, are usually already receiving outpatient treatment from the hospital, after a brief in-patient stay. They are often trying to return to what, at the time, they perceive as a secure or familiar environment.

Bizarre or mildly antisocial behaviour

Everyone reading this book will in all probability have seen a mentally ill person behaving strangely in a public place. Mumbling—or sometimes shouting insults or obscenities—at non-existent people, pacing repetitively as if enclosed in a small room, and so on. Sometimes these people will be freakishly dressed—the case studies we have included provide vivid examples—and they are almost uniformly unkempt, if not actually dirty in appearance. Very often they are clearly homeless or dependent on night shelters which make them return to the streets during the day.

We should stress immediately that not every such person will be schizophrenic. Many are acute alcoholics, whose behaviour results from a combination of intoxication and organic brain damage. Others may be mentally ill, but suffering from manic depression or other psychiatric disorders.

Some, however, will be schizophrenic and, regrettably, they may on occasions be detained by the police for a number of reasons. The degree to which certain forms of public behaviour are tolerated varies from culture to culture, as do the laws regarding the circumstances under which someone who is clearly mentally unstable can be forcibly hospitalized. Some schizophrenic people may commit petty offences, such as small-scale theft from shops. Often the lack of any attempt to conceal their action, or the utter uselessness of the items taken will quickly inform the police that their supposed criminal is in fact mentally ill.

Once this has been confirmed, a process may be initiated which ends with the person being sent to a hospital for diagnosis and reports. Later, we shall discuss the mechanism by which this enforced hospital admission can occur.

Assault and murder

Very rarely, a schizophrenic will seriously assault or even kill another person. There are numerous scenarios in which such events can occur, but it is generally true to say that such assaults are mostly carried out by patients with marked paranoid symptoms who have, for one reason or another, ceased to take their prescribed medication. (In the United Kingdom for example, over 80 per cent of people who kill their mothers fit this model.)

The other *classic scenario*, if such a word can be used to describe so distressing a phenomenon, involves the patient—again, usually paranoid or hearing voices, invariably from God, which command him to wreak vengeance on a particular group of people: homosexuals, prostitutes, or women generally. Many of the most notorious *mass* or *serial* murderers claim to have operated under divine mandate of some sort.

Although such assaults or murders invariably excite the tabloid news media to new depths of cruel, prurient, and garish hysteria, they are in fact extremely rare. Taking ordinary, single murders as an example, of the 550 or so committed in Britain in 1991, around 2 per cent were performed by diagnosed schizophrenics. As this tiny proportion suggests, schizophrenic patients are no more likely to commit murder than other people.

Attempted suicide

The patient who comes to treatment after committing an assault or a murder is highly unusual. The schizophrenic person who tries to harm or kill himself is, sadly, far more common. While it is unusual for a suicide attempt to pre-cipitate the patient's first encounter with the psychiatric services, it is a relatively frequent cause of repeated hospitalization.

The proportion of schizophrenic people, who at some time attempt suicide, is thought to be in the region of 30 per cent. This figure, despite the inclusion of the so-called *cry for help* pseudo-attempts common to the general pub-lic, is nonetheless disturbingly high. The number of schizophrenics who succeed in their attempt is also dis-proportionate to those in the community as a whole; it has been reported as being as high as one in ten, if one considers the developed world as a whole.

There is little one can say to ameliorate the impact of these figures, save that they act as an ever-present spur to researchers working to improve treatment methods for the disease, and that they serve to remind all those con-cerned with the illness of the vital importance of respond-ing to suicide threats from schizophrenics with the utmost seriousness and urgency.

Compulsory hospitalization

Every mental health-care system has some mechanism for admitting the severely disturbed or dangerous patient to hospital. These may differ in significant particulars from country to country. In very general terms: all systems allow for the enforced hospitalization of a patient who is a danger to others; most extend this power to include situations in which the patient is a danger to himself.

The moral dimension

The forcible incarceration of any individual, even in the healing environment of a hospital, necessarily poses serious questions of human rights. There is variation in the systems adopted by different countries which makes impossible a detailed presentation of the mechanisms that exist to protect the patient from an over-zealous or repressive system, but several principles are common to all responsible psychiatric regimes. Foremost among these is the principle that, after the safety of the public and the patient, the next most important consideration is the short- and long-term health and happiness of the person suffering from the illness. Last of all comes society's natural desire for basic standards of behaviour. If these principles are applied, the forcible hospitalization of certain schizophrenics seems justified.

Information concerning patients' rights is readily obtainable from a number of charities (SANE in the United Kingdom and the National Alliance for the Mentally Ill in the United States are particularly helpful) or, in some cases, from your family doctor.

Treatment on admission

The best way to illustrate a typical treatment regime for the newly admitted patient is to offer a fictional case study. In this way, we can have our imaginary patient behave in such a way as to illustrate the hospital's response to a variety of challenges that would rarely occur together in one case.

A fictional case study

Jamie, a 29-year-old man was brought to the Littleford hospital showing acute signs of mental disturbance. He lived alone in an extremely cluttered and dirty bed-sitting room, where police found him in a highly agitated state, bizarrely dressed, and screaming obscenities at an invisible person or persons. The neighbour who had called the police had done so reluctantly: she knew he was *very odd*, but found him likeable and had tried to help him in small ways throughout his tenancy there. On this occasion, however, he seemed out of control and she was scared to intervene, out of fear for her own safety. Jamie was known to be schizophrenic by the staff at the Littleford and had spent some time there a year previously as an in-patient.

On admission, Jamie was very disturbed. Having readily accepted the offer of a meal, he hurled the food at the orderly, accusing him of being a 'robot'. When he announced his intention to leave the hospital, the consulting psychiatrist on duty attempted to interview Jamie, only to be met with a mixture of verbiage (*word salad*) and grandiose threats of the 'I'll come back with a bomb and kill the lot of you' sort. The consultant decided that any attempts at further consultation were pointless until Jamie's aggressiveness had been quelled. At this point permission was granted for Jamie to be kept at the hospital and to be administered—by minimum force if necessary—a dose of chlorpromazine, a neuroleptic with pronounced sedative properties. This was achieved (with surprising ease) and Jamie even agreed to talk to the psychiatrist again in the morning.

When the morning arrived, many of Jamie's delusions and much of his aggressiveness had returned. He was initially polite in stating his intentions: he wished to leave hospital that day; he would not consider moving from orally taken to depot injected neuroleptics; he did not believe his behaviour presented a problem to himself or others. If these views were challenged, or even gently probed, he alternated between extreme anger and stubborn silence. Jamie was kept as calm as possible by the administration of the lowest effective dose of sedative medication, while the psychiatrist and her team met to develop a treatment plan—in which Jamie would himself have a role as soon as he felt able to discuss his state of mind more rationally.

The case meeting is usually chaired by the consultant psychiatrist. Its exact make-up will differ from country to country and from hospital to hospital, according to the prevailing system and the composition of the caring teams. At an appropriate point in the patient's treatment he, often together with a relative or close friend, will be invited to attend a case meeting. However, this is unlikely to occur while the patient is experiencing severe symptoms or is clearly unreceptive to the content of the meeting.

Surprisingly, given the animosity which characterized his admission and early treatment, Jamie's progress was extremely encouraging. He quickly regained his stable, albeit eccentric personality and, at his final case meeting, agreed to undertake a depot injection regime of neuroleptics, on the condition that he was accompanied to the clinic on the day in question by a psychiatric outreach worker (i.e. a nurse or social worker). While lack of resources make such arrangements very rare, it was agreed that Jamie would receive this form of support for three months, after which it would be reviewed. It was also agreed that he would be visited regularly by his social worker and that, should a psychiatric crisis occur, or Jamie feel the need for urgent qualified attention, the resources of the community psychiatric nurse would be readily available.

Long-term hospital care

Early discharge from hospital may not be possible for some patients. Their positive symptoms may not respond to ordinary doses of neuroleptics, or the side-effects may be so severe that constant regulation of doses or changes in medication are required. Some patients may need relatively lengthy preparation for discharge because they lack working skills or education. In many cases, patients are financially poor and lack the funds to resettle in the community. Others have long-standing negative schizophrenic symptoms with occasional relapses of positive symptoms; even after the latter have been relieved by neuroleptic treatment, the continuing presence of negative symptoms will prevent their early reintegration into the community.

There are, of course, problems attached to long-term hospital care. The longer a patient has been in hospital, the less likely it is that he will want to leave. Lengthy hospital stays can exacerbate negative symptoms and cause the *institutionalization* syndrome, manifested by loss of interest and initiative, lack of individuality, submissiveness, and a deterioration of personal habits. It is therefore important to minimize the patient's stay in hospital after the initial phase of positive symptoms has passed. Unless there are exceptional factors present, the earlier the discharge, the better. The patient's relatives and possibly working life is less disrupted and he does not associate the hospital with sanity and the outside world with frightening chaos, as can happen to long-stay patients. We have already seen that in extreme cases, this feeling can become so pronounced that the patient repeatedly seeks re-admission to his perceived *safe haven*, even making pseudo-suicide attempts or faking psychotic behaviour in order to return.

Of course, this policy can be carried too far. We have already seen some of the tragic effects of the inappropriately early release of certain schizophrenics into the community.

Section 4

Caring and coping in a changing social environment

Introduction

Every central government worships uniformity: uniformity relieves it from inquiry into an infinity of details, which must be attended to if rules have to be adapted to different men, instead of indiscriminately subjecting all men to the same rule.

De Tocqueville: *Democracy in America* 1835

Kinship is healing; we are physicians to each other.

Oliver Sacks: *Awakenings* 1973

Society and social structures are dynamic. Technological advances alone ensure that little remains the same for very long. Indeed, the extreme pace of scientifically driven social change is arguably *the* defining characteristic of the late-twentieth century. Yet for all that, scientific invention and research have served to benefit the schizophrenic person, it cannot be said to have completely eradicated all the problems sufferers face. To tender just one example: neuroleptic drugs, despite their benefits, still produce an unacceptable range of side-effects and one cannot guarantee that they will prevent relapse in a large number of patients.

This is not to decry or debase the role of scientific and clinical research into schizophrenia. We are, rather, emphasizing that the help and assistance that most patients need on a continuing basis will, of necessity, be provided by *people* starting with themselves and including their relatives and friends, members of the caring professions and, ultimately, by society as a whole.

In the following chapters, we shall first consider some of the problems faced by schizophrenics in their daily lives and at the ways in which some if not all of these may be alleviated with the help of those mentioned above. In doing so, we must keep in mind that there are patients for whom no amount of external help will materially affect the course of their illness.

We shall then look at the issue of prognosis (outcome) for those with schizophrenia and examine some of the medical, social, and cultural factors that appear to affect the outcome of the illness.

16
What special problems does the schizophrenic person face?

Problems caused by features of the schizophrenic brain

In Section Two of this book, we asked 'Is schizophrenia a disease of the brain?' As we examined the evidence relating to this question, we saw that, when subjected to neuropsychological tests, schizophrenics exhibited poor attention and difficulty in concentrating on one thing at a time. They often found it hard to form concepts or to think abstractly, and many had a problem remembering things.

It is immediately obvious that anyone with these difficulties will find it hard to cope with some of the ordinary demands of life. If the patient is also experiencing the still more debilitating, although sometimes intermittent, positive and negative symptoms of schizophrenia described in Section One of this book, his mental problems can make the barriers to a normal life seem insuperable. Let us see if this is really the case with regard to specific problems many schizophrenics face.

Employment

This is an area of particular difficulty for those with schizophrenia. We have already noted that for a great many sufferers, work of any kind is a practical impossibility; the severity of their symptoms and the chaotic pattern that their lives have followed combine to make the demands of even the simplest work unrealistically high. For another group, the almost constant presence of less visible symptoms—usually negative—will also make most forms of work impossible.

Avolition, the lack of 'get up and go' required to seek work in the first place, may be so pronounced that the schizophrenic patient literally wants to be left alone with his (disordered) thoughts. In an increasingly competitive world, the prospective candidate who cannot demonstrate a keen desire to perform the work on offer has next to no chance of gaining employment.

We have also noted in the section on negative symptoms, problems such as *affective flattening* (emotional blunting) and *poverty of speech*. The result of these symptoms is to make the patient appear apathetic, inarticulate, and less intelligent than is probably the case. Again, none of these characteristics are likely to impress the prospective employer.

There is little to be gained by enumerating the 'symptoms of schizophrenia as barriers to employment'. The reader's common sense will suggest a myriad ways in which difficulties can arise. However, a word should be said about people with special forms of schizophrenia. Where the person in question experiences symptoms of the illness only very intermittently, or is suffering a closely related condition, such as schizotypal personality disorder, the issue of employment may become still more problematic. Whereas the severely ill schizophrenic is clearly incapable of work, the family and carers of less acutely affected sufferers may feel that they should be *persuaded* to work, if only to avoid the effects of poverty. This can lead to a stressful and miserable existence, and a marked worsening in the person's general condition.

If a schizophrenic sufferer is over-challenged or caused stress by the nature of the job (e.g. commission-only selling), the net result is likely to be negative.

How sufferers can help themselves

Sufferers from schizophrenia should not allow themselves to be goaded into taking a job about which they feel anxious or scared. Just as most schizophrenics learn how to avoid over- or under-stimulating situations in other aspects of their lives, they must try to apply this to prospective jobs. In addition, they must learn to recognize the *right* way of making choices concerning their future. This will be to some extent a matter of trial and error, but most sufferers who enjoy periods of relative or complete remission learn to reserve important decision-making for those times whenever possible. Certainly, decisions should not be made on the advice of voices heard in one's head, even if they seem to be offering relevant and common sense advice.

However close the person's relationship may be with his family or care givers, nobody suffering from schizophrenia should take as large a step as accepting a job simply to please them. If reservations about work exist, they should be aired in calm and reasonable circumstances, and not hidden in the hope of showing enthusiasm and concealing genuine worries.

What relatives can do

Although we say 'relatives', in the majority of cases, the parents are most likely to find themselves involved in caring for the schizophrenic, particularly where onset is early, with the sufferer still in college or a first job. Brothers, sisters, aunts and uncles, and even grandparents may all have something to contribute, but we shall be concentrating here mainly on parents. In some obvious cases the words 'parent' and 'close relative' are interchangeable.

It should also be noted that parents are more likely than other relatives unwittingly to provide *obstacles* to recovery, usually by reason of their living in the same house as the sufferer. They may, as a result become 'over-engaged' in their child's problems or react too quickly and emotionally to problems which quiet time alone would rapidly alleviate. Additionally, some parents may think of their children as extensions of themselves and hold vicarious ambitions for their sons and daughters.

It is among the most natural of all parental ambitions to see a child happily settled in a satisfying job. The prospect of having a son or daughter who will never work is—quite apart from the financial implications—a demoralizing one for many parents to face. With work comes all the other normal features of 'growing up': financial independence, house-ownership, marriage, and eventually, the next generation of children. Some young people experience one bout of the illness and recover completely, never to be troubled by it again, but these are relatively rare. Few schizophrenics who experience early onset progress through all these rites of passage without some problems along the way.

Parental reactions when faced with this deeply saddening situation can vary widely; some immediately begin the search for someone to blame, often starting with themselves. This helps no one and is counter-productive in the extreme. Others, on learning of the diagnosis of schizophrenia, immediately throw themselves into learning all they can about the illness, reading books and contacting charities in order to find out what they can do to help. This activity, if conducted in a calm and constructive manner is very commendable, but there is the danger that parents, equipped with a good lay person's knowledge of schizophrenia, will try to become counsellors for their son or daughter, taking upon themselves decisions or ideas regarding the possibility of work. This kind of intervention, however well-intentioned, may not be truly helpful in the long term. Where work is concerned, parents *can* best assist their children by ensuring that the doctor assigned to their child's care is aware of and approves any positive action undertaken.

It is especially vital that parents never goad a child into taking a job, for reasons of finance. 'After all we've done for you ...' may work with a person who is simply lazy, but should never be used to create a feeling of guilt in a schizophrenic child. The results of this kind of remark vary from simply reinforcing the sufferer's feelings of persecution, to precipitating full-scale family breakdown; rarely, if ever, is anything positive achieved for either party.

Lastly, parents may need to readjust their expectations of their children quite dramatically. In some cases, this will demand that they recognize the impossibility of their child working at all in the foreseeable future. For others, it will entail discarding their assumption that their children were destined for 'high-flying' professions. It may seem a terrible waste of talent to see someone with a first-class honours degree working on a factory floor, but if that is what the schizophrenic person feels comfortable doing, he should be congratulated and encouraged for being willing and able to do so.

One particularly productive line of research into the family environment of schizophrenic patients has examined 'expressed emotion' (EE). The original UK study by Dr Julian Leff from London, defined EE in terms of the number of critical comments, the amount of hostility, and the degree of emotional over-involvement that the family directed toward the patient. They measured EE by interviewing family members about the patients. These interviews were tape-recorded so that they could be examined in detail for comments that would indicate the presence of EE. After extensive scorings of these recordings, researchers divided families into high-expressed emotion (High EE) and low-expressed emotion (Low EE) groups.

A series of studies investigated a total of 128 schizophrenic patients who lived with their families. After classifying the families as either high EE or low EE, the researchers kept track of the patients to see who would relapse (when the condition of patients worsens we say that they have relapsed). Thirteen per cent of patients (9 of 71) from Low EE families relapsed after 9 months. In the High EE families, 51 per cent (29 of 57) relapsed over a 9-month period. In the High EE group, relapse rates were 29 per cent for those patients who had spent less than 35 hours per week in face-to-face contact with the family; 69 per cent of patients who had more contact with their patients relapsed. Thus, it appears that patients who live with families that are critical, hostile, and over-involved are at increased risk for relapse. This finding emphasizes the importance of family therapy programmes aimed at reducing EE in the families of schizophrenic patients.

It is important to recognize another possible inter-pretation of studies that examine EE in families of schizo-phrenic patients. Instead of concluding that EE causes schizophrenic relapse, it is possible that the re-emergence of schizophrenic symptoms (which precede a relapse) creates increased levels of EE in the family. Thus, symp-toms prior to relapse might cause both EE and the subse-quent relapse.

So what should families make of the EE studies? In our view, it seems reasonable to assume that a complex series of events leads to schizophrenic relapse. These events include non-compliance with medication, stressful life events, and adverse social interactions with friends, employers, and family members. However, it is also likely that schizophrenic symptoms can set the stage for each of the elements of the relapse process. As symptoms re-emerge, patients are less likely to take their medication and their psychotic behaviour may create stressful events. Moreover, their behaviour will be increasingly stressful to others, who in turn, may become more hostile, critical, or over-involved.

Thus, increasing symptoms and increasing EE may be part of a spiral of events that lead to relapse. It makes no sense to worry about which caused which first. This is a 'chicken and egg' question that has little relevance to the lives of schizophrenic patients and their families. The crucial point is that patients and their relatives understand this spiral so that they can try to stop it before a full relapse occurs

What the caring services can do

One might assume that a country, having asserted its determination to see the mentally ill take their rightful place within the community, would do something to ensure that they take their place as *employed* citizens. At present, apart from the admirable efforts of over-stretched and under-resourced charities, little real help exists to help schizophrenics find work. Often the person's social worker will put him in touch with a charity or organization that is known to be effective in this area.

In the United Kingdom and the United States, the state, together with charities, provides a measure of 'sheltered work' for the mentally ill and handicapped people and this might be considered as a useful stepping stone for the recovering schizophrenic who does not feel ready to enter the faster-moving world of private commerce immediately. Some local authorities and private companies have policies of maintaining a certain percentage of mentally ill or handicapped people within their workforce; specialist charities can help to identify these.

What employers can do

It is almost redundant to remind the reader of the public prejudice directed against those with mental illnesses, and schizophrenia especially. We believe that this can and will diminish in time, if only in the way that scientific progress has to date, increased understanding of many illnesses leading to greater sympathy with those who suffer from them. In the meantime, however, the schizophrenic job-hunter will be fortunate not to encounter prejudice in this, as in so many other areas of his life.

Most of the bodies which represent people with mental illnesses ask only that the prospective employer presented with someone who has experienced episodes of schizophrenia looks not at the illness but at the *person* and his suitability for the job. They are not demanding special concessions, merely asking for an absence of prejudice. If there is uncertainty about a person's ability to do the work on health grounds a reference should be requested that names the psychiatrist who is currently treating the applicant. You can thus be sure of receiving an honest assessment of the person's abilities, the magnitude of which may surprise you.

Social security and welfare benefits

In almost all developed countries some financial provision is made for those who are unable to work by reason of physical or mental sickness. These systems of provision are usually huge bureaucracies and the potential recipient must understand complex rules, fill in numerous forms, and maintain regular contact with a designated office if he is to receive benefit. As with the demands of employment and job-seeking, it is hard to imagine a set of tasks more challenging to the schizophrenic person. The avolition of which we wrote with reference to employment is likely to be every bit as disabling where seeking benefit payment is concerned.

What the patient can do

The most that the patient can do to help himself in this situation is to ensure that he is actually receiving the sum to which he is entitled. If this means bringing a friend or family member with him to interviews, this should be arranged. If the benefits office objects, a letter should be obtained from the psychiatrist or social worker concerned explaining the necessity for this procedure.

How the benefits service can help

Many public employment agencies the world over employ someone with special responsibility for people with disabilities of all kinds, including mental illness. With their own resources often stretched to the limits, it may help those with this responsibility to make use of some of the excellent, and usually free, literature on schizophrenia available from organizations which specialize in helping schizophrenic people generally; most will at least offer basic guidelines on dealing with schizophrenic people seeking work. In both the United Kingdom and the United States, several charities exist which produce specialist material of this kind.

Some of these charities run their own workshops and training schemes, aimed at helping the sufferer into work. Several have telephone helplines and are willing to do everything within their power to assist bodies such as Job Centres to amass databases, receive newsletters, and so on.

Homelessness

The breakdown of family relationships or a simple urge to isolate oneself socially can all too quickly lead to homelessness. SANE estimates that some 40 per cent of homeless people suffer mental illness of some kind; many of these will be schizophrenics.

Once homeless, the vicious cycle of downward social drift rapidly manifests itself. With no address, one can only apply for limited state help; job-hunting becomes impossible because one's appearance immediately gives one away as an 'indigent', and one can probably not afford to travel to interviews anyway. Actively shunned or simply out of touch with former friends, the sufferer may wander utterly alone or take up with the 'street people', found in every sizeable town or city. Mainly alcoholics, drug addicts, and other mentally disturbed people, their company, however welcome at the time, is rarely conducive to recovery. As a matter of plain fact, many schizophrenics *do* at some point in their lives lack shelter. Can anything be done to prevent this?

Can patients and their parents or close family avoid this problem?

In some, though by no means all cases, the schizophrenic living rough on the street is doing so because life at home has become intolerable for all parties. Just as many juveniles run away following family arguments or simply owing to a sense of confinement, some schizophrenics feel that they must leave home either in response to some major precipitating event or to an accumulated sense of being 'closed in' or 'trapped'. There, unfortunately, the comparison ceases to be of use. Many young runaways act in a fit of rage which progressively dissipates as they face up to the realities of life on cold, inhospitable streets. Alternatively, their action may be intended as a warning to their parents, intended to alter power relationships within the family structure. It is true that many do not return quickly, or in some cases at all, but the reasons for their leaving are at least rational. Schizophrenic individuals, in contrast, may be operating from a different and far from rational set of premises. They may have left home to escape terrifying hallucinations brought on by a family argument, or under the paranoid delusion that their parents are steadily poisoning them by adding small quantities of powdered glass to their food.

A further problem exists in the fact that the split may be mutual. No one's patience is inexhaustible, and parents who have repeatedly experienced the most bizarre or troublesome behaviour of a son or daughter suffering schizophrenic symptoms may finally 'snap'. If the schizophrenic chooses this moment to leave the house, a parent may make no attempt to intervene.

There are, however, some ways of calming confrontations if—and this is a large *if*—both parties are able to refrain even for a few moments from acting on impulse. Those who work with schizophrenics continually stress the necessity to initiate and maintain a calm atmosphere, particularly when discussing subjects that experience has shown may exacerbate the condition. It is also well established that the usual solution for family problems, namely talking them through, may actually make matters worse for the schizophrenic: *confronting* one's mental problems is by no means always helpful, and should ideally be undertaken in the presence of a psychiatrist, psychologist, or other qualified health professional.

It is usually true to say that a sufferer who abruptly leaves home has been experiencing symptoms for some time. Hence, the best preventive action that families can take is to be alert to signs of these symptoms and persuade the patient to see the doctor before matters reach crisis point. We shall have more to say on this issue later but a few of these 'pointers to crisis' can be mentioned here.

The first rule is to remember that the patient will not always be truthful about his state of mind. Do not let this distress you; rather accept it and make allowance for it. Hallucinations can sometimes be detected. Sudden eye movements, laughter, or agitation may all be evidence of their presence. Patients seem more prone to denying that they are hearing voices than other symptoms. Again, sudden outbursts of laughter or snatches of speech—occasionally obscene—may indicate the hearing of voices. Also, one should be alert to *subvocalization*, that is very quiet muttering or even soundless word formation: the subvocalizing patient is often responding to his voices.

Paranoid delusions may be difficult to detect, since the person feels it to be imperative that his perceived persecutors do not know that their 'plot' has been discovered. The most visible signs of paranoid delusions are changes in routine which, although innocent, may point to deepseated problems. If a son who has always been content to eat with the family, requests that he eat in his room, suddenly refuses lifts in the car or exhibits marked discomfort in the presence of a certain family member, it may be that there are delusions attached to these variables. As one can imagine, they can be almost impossible to detect.

The same cannot be said of the second most common clue to delusions. Some patients, suffering extreme paranoia, may try to defend themselves from destructive forces by adding protective materials or talismans to their clothing, performing pseudo-magical rituals, or speaking in 'invented languages'. As a general rule, radical changes in behaviour, however harmless in themselves, may be pointers to severe underlying problems. Medical help should be sought immediately.

With regard to homelessness in general, the most important principle for families to bear in mind is that persuading sufferers to return home may become increasingly difficult the longer they have lived on the streets. Social isolation is attractive to many schizophrenics, and if they are living rough the chances are that they will manifest schizophrenic preferences because of the little likelihood of their receiving properly monitored medication. Also, some schizophrenics are very prone to the formation of routines such as standing outside one shop for two hours, spending an hour in the launderette, walking up and down a certain road at a certain time, and so on. Once these routines—which may have a calming effect on the sufferer—are established, it may be hard to persuade him to renounce them.

Housing

In the scenarios considered earlier the schizophrenic person was living rough as a result of leaving home and, with the exception we noted, the possibility of returning *did* exist. It need hardly be said that this is not the case where many schizophrenics are concerned. Older sufferers, in particular, are likely to have arrived on the streets following discharge from a mental institution, or following the breakdown of a marriage. Some may have additional problems, such as alcoholism, which have combined with their illness to make life with them impossible in a domestic setting. They will simply sleep rough, either alone or joining other down-and-outs in city parks and the pathetic 'cardboard cities' that now blight so many large cities.

Where is the homeless schizophrenic person to find lasting help?

We are not suggesting that there is no provision for someone needing a bed for the night. Most local authorities and many charities run night shelters or short-stay hostels for the homeless. Some sufferers, if they are lucky and the resources exist, may be found permanent accommodation in a council-owned flat or house. The real problem lies in finding adequate places for increasing numbers of homeless people, whether mentally ill or not.

The schizophrenic person living rough on the streets faces a truly grim existence. Even at the bottom end of the scale, the 'night-only' hostels which residents must vacate each morning will sometimes refuse the schizophrenic person admission because of his unpredictable behaviour, such as shouting out in the night.

The lack of adequate accommodation for unemployed schizophrenics is one of the greatest problems facing carers and sufferers alike. Although in theory no patient should be discharged from hospital simply to roam the streets, anyone not admitted by a court order is at liberty to discharge himself.

Drugs and alcohol

The abuse of drugs and alcohol is to some extent a further consequence of the downward social spiral already described. While it is perfectly true that people in close and stable families or with caring and responsible friends *do* suffer these problems, they are far more pronounced among those living rough, in cities particularly. Even if the homeless schizophrenic has never drunk excessively or experimented with drugs, he may well find that his new acquaintances on the streets are hardened alcoholics or drug-users.

The problems that drugs and drink can cause the schizophrenic fall essentially into three categories. First, there are the problems common to all those who drink excessively. Their health is likely to suffer considerably; they are more prone to accidents and violent assault as a result of arguments; and in some countries they are breaking the law by drinking in public, and may be tempted into more serious crime. Finally, their appearance and behaviour is likely to deteriorate, making it still less likely that they will find work, or be welcomed back into their families. If they are involved with drugs, the effects will be broadly similar but, owing to the high price of drugs, the effect on their already meagre finances will often be disastrous.

The second problem relates specifically to schizophrenics, many of whom find the mind-altering effects of alcohol and drugs extremely pleasant. Whether these chemicals really do provide a genuine respite from some of the symptoms of schizophrenia is unlikely, but there is no doubt that some sufferers show a sufficient affinity for drink or some types of drug to become seriously addicted. Known colloquially to mental health workers as 'double trouble patients', they often meet serious problems if in-patient care is required for them.

We have already mentioned that alcohol and illicit drugs may cause potentially dangerous effects in schizophrenic people. It is, finally, worth mentioning that the same can be said of some drugs obtained quite innocently across the pharmacist's counter. Many proprietary medicines contain substances which can cause violent reactions in schizophrenic patients. Among these ingredients are ephedrine, pseudoephedrine, hyoscine, and diphenhydramine, which may be found in preparations for nasal blockage, wheezing, travel sickness, and hay fever, respectively. This is by no means a complete list. These are simply a few examples of drugs which may cause reactions in the schizophrenic patient; any medication not already prescribed by a doctor should be checked with him before use. The problem for the isolated, homeless, or already intoxicated person is that he may well have lost contact with his doctor, and even for the purpose of receiving the neuroleptic drugs he needs to stay well.

How the patient can help himself

The typical schizophrenic learns most about the effect of specific situations on his state of mind by trial and error, avoiding those which either over- or under-stimulate him. The same method can be applied to the use of specific substances, whether they are entirely benign, such as new kinds of food, or potentially hazardous, such as alcohol.

The physical effects of excessive use of alcohol are exactly the same for the schizophrenic as for anyone else. The special dangers for schizophrenics of using any mind- or mood-altering substance that we have described (alcohol included) may in themselves be sufficient to deter the sufferer from experimentation with them. These dangers, of course, have first to be communicated and that duty in practice, falls to others.

Where the patient *can* do most to help himself is in ensuring that he takes his own prescribed medication correctly and that he does not accidentally consume un-prescribed over-the-counter preparations, however innocuous their name and packaging might imply. Given the enormous number of patent preparations containing similar, but in not every case identical chemicals, it may be very difficult to know whether a medicine is safe to be taken. The following checklist covers most situations in which drug-related problems might occur:

(1) Where taking your own medication is concerned, devise a set routine in conjunction with your doctor and, if possible, a family member who can be present

to double-check the procedure if required. Try to learn and remember the names and purposes of the drugs, in case you take too many by accident or miss a dose.

(2) Obtain a medical card which carries details of your condition and your normal medication on it. Your doctor will give you one or help you get one. If you really do not wish to carry such a card, at least keep a clearly written list of the drugs you are currently receiving, including the dosages, with you at all times. Have your doctor or psychiatric nurse check the list for accuracy.

(3) Always use the same pharmacy or chemist. Your doctor should contact the pharmacist in advance if you are going to receive your drugs there regularly. Some chemists operate a card-system or computerized database, so that whichever branch you visit, they will know all they need to about your medication regime.

(4) If you are going to buy a patent preparation for a specific condition—a sore throat or a cold, perhaps—always check its suitability with the pharmacist. If a temporary pharmacist is serving, or if you are compelled to use another chemist, do not make your purchase before speaking to the pharmacist and explaining that you suffer from schizophrenia. You may find this process intimidating; if so, simply show him your medical card or the list of drugs you are already receiving.

(5) Never accept offers of other people's medicines, however much they tell you that they cannot harm you. The likelihood is that they know nothing whatsoever about the possible interactions between complex chemicals.

(6) By the same token, never offer your drugs to others. A substance which serves to calm you down and relax you may have a violently different effect on someone else.

How parents, friends, and carers can help

We have grouped these three categories of people together because, according to the particular circumstances
of the patient's life, one or other will see him most often
and will be best placed to monitor his mood and behaviour. There will be instances when, despite the patient's
living at home, it will be a friend or social worker who first
notices that drink or drugs are being misused.

The first important thing that those close to the
patient can do is to recognize that the problem *could* exist.
People who are ill may do things that are quite out of
character with their 'well' self. Hence, the fact that the
person in question has never before shown any interest in
drink or drugs should not be taken as certain grounds for
their current abstinence.

There are few hard and fast rules concerning the use of
alcohol among schizophrenics. If the patient is in remission, and has a history of moderate, social drinking, his
doctor may not consider continued light use to be dangerous. Few neuroleptic drugs list ordinary alcohol use
among their **contraindications** (i.e. substances with or
situations in which the drug must not be used). Family,
friends, and others close to the sufferer should discuss this
matter with the doctor if possible to ascertain his policy.
Do not simply be content with the patient's claim that
'the doctor said it was OK'.

Generally speaking, the person caring for a schizophrenic relative, friend or client is similarly placed to
parents who are concerned about a child taking drugs or
the spouse who suspects an alcoholic wife or husband of
secret drinking. There are numerous 'clues' of which one
should be aware. We cannot list them here, but all doctor's offices and psychiatric hospitals have numerous
invaluable leaflets covering these subjects.

The main difference where the schizophrenic is
concerned lies in the degree of sensitivity required in
handling these situations, and in the severity of the

reaction if the sufferer feels 'spied on'. No teenager likes to find his mother looking under his bed for drug paraphernalia, just as an alcoholic may explode with righteous anger when his secret whisky cache is discovered. Generally, however, the matter will be forgotten sooner or later.

In contrast, the schizophrenic who feels—rightly in this case—that his movements are being scrutinized, his room searched when he is out and so on, may be projected into a state of full-blown paranoia. It is, therefore, important that any discussion of the problem should take place in a calm and open atmosphere. It is important not to 'confront' the sufferer with the evidence of his drinking or drug use; this will probably be unnecessary in any case.

You may find that your doctor or psychiatrist feels unable to intervene unless expressly approached by the patient himself. This is a common problem affecting many other aspects of schizophrenia, but it need not be insuperable as we shall see later. Several charities have helplines staffed by qualified counsellors who will gladly do what they can to advise and assist you about the most sensible way to deal with the problem.

Difficulties with social interaction and communication

Most schizophrenics soon discover that certain forms of social interaction are liable to precipitate serious symptoms such as delusions and hallucinations. Examples of these experiences include heated arguments about religion or politics, emotional 'scenes' or discussions with the family, situations conducive to day-dreaming or fantasizing, and exposure to large crowds of people.

Obviously, the simplest way of avoiding these is to isolate oneself socially, but to do so may be to court other problems; some schizophrenics only hear voices when they are alone and this as we know, may be extremely disturbing. This aside, the isolated sufferer is less likely to adhere to a medication regime and may over a period of time, lose all sense of social orientation.

Many schizophrenics find it exceptionally difficult to communicate with 'authority figures'. In a clinical setting, this may have significant results; a simple inability to inarticulate in the face of a professional figure, such as a general practitioner, may be perceived as evidence of a greater degree of poverty of content of speech or thought withdrawal than is actually the case. In an ideal world no doctor would fail to make such a seemingly simple mistake. However, under a system in which many general practitioners are so over-worked that they must limit all ordinary consultations to ten minutes, one can see how easily these clues can be overlooked.

Are these problems insuperable? Who can help?

We have already mentioned that schizophrenic people themselves are frequently capable of deciding which situations aggravate their symptoms and which do not. In much the same way they can frequently identify those forms of communication, such as group discussions, which they find difficult to manage.

Let us first consider patients who have acute difficulty communicating well in a medical setting. They may feel extremely anxious simply being in a hospital or doctor's office, perhaps because of a negative association with a previous visit or stay or because hospitals play a part in a particular paranoid delusion. There is a genuine risk that rather than subject themselves to an appointment, they will forgo regular meetings with their general practitioner, thereby failing to receive their medication, either via prescription or as a depot injection.

The patient's ability to overcome this problem is obviously limited. However, as in all matters relating to schizophrenia, the important thing is to try to communicate the difficulty to someone whom one trusts. If a family member, close friend, or psychiatric nurse knows of the problem, and *why* the reluctance exists, there is at least the potential for remedial action to be taken.

The most obvious and natural strategy to cope with this obstacle, if the patient is willing, is for one of the above to accompany him to the consultation. Many psychiatrists have mixed feelings about this, and for good reasons, but it should be considered if only as an interim arrangement whereby the third-party offers support and 'translates' the patient's more arcane utterances, until the clinician himself can build a working relationship with the sufferer. The mere fact of knowing that *somebody* present at an assessment knows and understands the patient personally will more often than not make for a more productive and mutually comprehensible encounter.

Keeping problems in perspective

Celebrate success!

Rome was not built in a day. Yet every stone, column, court, and villa that composed this glorious city could metaphorically fit inside just a pinch of the grey matter that composes the true miracle of the human brain. Its complexity continues to astound our most brilliant scientists and the harmony with which it operates can prompt the most hardened atheists into a sense of near-spiritual wonder.

When science achieves neurological breakthroughs, we justly celebrate them, and in doing so provide a spur for further achievement. Should we not celebrate with equal vigour when just one brain is involved? We know how difficult many everyday operations are for schizophrenics to accomplish: remembering a new medication regime or appointment time, performing some task unaided with which one had formerly required help, or successfully employing a new strategy to keep symptoms at bay. For the schizophrenic individual these are genuine achievements and should be treated as such. We must not forget the value to the confidence of the patient and the morale of the caring team that jointly achieved accomplishments represent. In psychiatry, as in all things, success begets success.

17

Prognosis

Every night and every morn
Some to misery are born;
Every morn and every night
Some are born to sweet delight;
Some are born to sweet delight,
Some are born to endless night.

William Blake: *Proverbs*

I am not fond of the word psychological. There is no such thing as psychological. Let us say that one can improve the biography of the person.

Attributed to Jean-Paul Sartre

What can patients expect from their future?

Although we have examined some of the ways in which problems caused by schizophrenia may be alleviated, the illness itself sets limits on the progress that is possible in each person's case. Put bluntly, some people suffer it more acutely and intractably than others. However one manipulates and amends the system that exists to treat schizophrenia, not every patient will reap the full benefits of treatment. Complete recovery will be out of the question for many and the most one can do for them will be to ensure that they are as well cared for as possible for as long as is necessary.

Let us look at the issue of prognosis and at the statistical guides we have as to the likely outcome of the illness for schizophrenic individuals as a group.

It is important that the reader clearly understands the distinction between **course** and **prognosis**, since the terms and subjects are frequently considered successively.

Course refers to the way in which the illness manifests itself through time (i.e. throughout the patient's life). A typical course of an individual's illness might be an acute onset in the early twenties, followed by periods of remission in which only a few negative symptoms are present, but punctuated by occasional acute relapses.

Prognosis, in psychiatric terminology, refers to predicting course and outcome; it forecasts the likelihood of the patient recovering from the illness, although this need not entail a complete recovery. Similarly, it need not refer to the patient's entire life; merely to the duration of a particular study. We might say someone's 'outcome was fair' at the follow-up to a ten-year study, without intending any extrapolation to be made regarding his future progress.

This flexibility of usage is entirely in keeping with the unpredictable nature of schizophrenia. Unlike certain forms of physical illness, the clinician can rarely say with certainty that something will or will not happen within a given period of time, or indeed at all.

Studies of prognosis

Numerous clinical research projects have been conducted to identify which factors appear to point to good or bad prognosis in schizophrenia. The results of these studies into outcome have varied considerably. There have been cases where this variation was due at least in part to the kind of schizophrenia that was being studied. In others, factors such as how long the patients were observed, and how outcome was assessed may have been responsible. In still other cases, no reasons could be identified for the variations.

This lack of agreement, together with the complex relationships between the factors that must in fact affect outcome, make it extremely difficult to generalize about prognosis. A brief overview of the most prominent research projects into the subject confirms the lack of anything approaching complete unanimity on the rates, if not the factors, affecting prognosis in schizophrenia. It does, however, open the door to possibilities which are in themselves intriguing. Further study into these possibilities is an exciting prospect. There may be much to tell us not only about outcome in schizophrenia, but about the nature of the illness and our responses to it.

Kraepelinian schizophrenia

You may recall from Section One that *Kraepelin* stressed irrecoverable mental deterioration when separating schizophrenia from typical manic-depressive illness. He used a diagnostic term 'dementia praecox', to characterize this relatively narrow concept of schizophrenia: namely, an illness which usually took place during or shortly after adolescence with life-long mental deterioration. Subsequently, he changed his definition, so that complete recovery was not incompatible with a diagnosis of the illness.

Using his latterly adopted concept of schizophrenia, the number of patients who recovered completely was still very low, at 2.6 per cent. He conducted a range of such studies and reported rates of lasting recovery ranging from 0 to 5.5 per cent.

Subsequent studies have shown a wider variation in good outcome. The figures themselves, which range from 11 to 66 per cent are less important than the discovery that the broader the definition of schizophrenia used, the more favourable the outcome. (A 'broad' definition of the illness would include patients with mild symptoms only or with prominent mood disorder in addition to schizophrenia.) In general, the longer the follow-up period in studies of patients, the worse the outcome.

Naturally, studies made after the discovery of neuro-leptic medicines show better outcome than previous ones. However, even generalizations of this sort need qualification. Standard methods of research must be used to test each assumption by taking into account all factors which may influence the results, something which has yet to be accomplished with regard to schizophrenia. It is, however, worth reviewing concisely some of the studies conducted, and to illustrate the difficulties involved in administering outcome studies. The method we shall adopt to do this will be to identify the research, its basic methodology and conclusions, and briefly to state and evaluate its reliability and enduring relevance to modern psychiatry, if any.

Dr *Manfred Bleuler*, son of Dr Eugen Bleuler who coined the term 'schizophrenia', reported a long-term study of 208 schizophrenics. Twenty years after their first hospitalization, complete remission had occurred in 20 per cent of patients; mild symptoms persisted in 33 per cent; and a severe defect in 47 per cent. Forty-three per cent of the patients were living outside an institution, completely or partly self-supporting. Only 10 per cent had no subsequent hospital admissions after discharge, and another 10 per cent remained in hospital following re-admission. A total of 6 per cent continued in hospital without ever being discharged. The remaining 73 per cent had more than one subsequent admission and discharge.

Although Bleuler listed eight key characteristics for diagnosing schizophrenia, no specific diagnostic criteria were used to select his sample. We cannot, therefore, be certain what sort of schizophrenia he studied. Moreover, the 'defects' he mentioned in respect to outcome were never objectively defined. These omissions make his results difficult to interpret, but there is much to be gleaned from what remains one of the most comprehensive long-term outcome studies conducted to date.

Another study conducted by *Luc Ciompi* at the Psychiatric University Hospital of Lausanne, Switzerland selected a total of 289 patients born between 1873 and 1897, so that lifelong information, at least up to the age of

65, could be obtained at follow-up interviews with all who survived.

The results obtained were remarkably similar to Bleuler's. After an average of 37 years from first admission to re-examination, the results of outcome were classified as follows: 27 per cent, complete remission; 22 per cent, some minor symptoms; 42 per cent, unfavourable outcome or severe defects; the remaining 9 per cent, either uncertain or unstable. At the time of follow-up, 40 per cent of patients were living either with their families or by themselves; the rest were either in hospitals or community institutions. The mean age of the patients at follow-up was 74; nevertheless, 51 per cent were still working; two-thirds in part-time and one-third in full-time jobs.

The similarity with Bleuler's results may be due to certain selective factors—deceased patients obviously could not be interviewed, and those who came to interview had clearly enjoyed relatively good outcomes. From these results we can conclude that schizophrenia, defined according to Bleuler's concept, tends to show better outcome than that defined by the narrower version attributable to Kraepelin.

Dr Eric Steinberg at the Institute of Psychiatry of the Academy of Medical Sciences in Moscow has shown that many of the chronic features of schizophrenia stabilize or disappear in schizophrenics, particularly women, over the age of 60, allowing as many as 38 per cent to live outside hospital. These outcome studies from Europe and the former Soviet Union suggest a more positive outcome for schizophrenia than had been previously supposed.

The Iowa Study was conducted by a team of researchers led by *Dr Ming Tsuang*, now at Harvard University. This research, which reported a 30- to 40-year study of the outcome of schizophrenia in 1979 in Iowa sought to overcome some of the deficiencies and bias of those previously described. Two hundred schizophrenics, who met the Washington University research criteria, were selected from consecutive admissions to the University of Iowa Psychiatric Hospital between 1934 and 1944. In addition, 325 patients with mood disorders (bipolar disorder or depression), and 160 surgical patients, who had undergone appendix or hernia operations, were selected as controls. The manic-depressive patients had been admitted by the same psychiatric hospital during the same period as the schizophrenics. They were included to allow a comparison of outcome.

Traditionally, the outcome of mood disorder is assumed to be better than that of schizophrenia. The surgical patients were included to test whether the outcome of non-psychiatric patients was in any way different from that of psychiatric patients. In order not to prejudice the study, follow-up information was collected without the collectors knowing the diagnostic group to which each patient belonged.

A total of 97 per cent of patients were successfully traced at follow-up, including those who had died. Using structured interview forms, outcome data was collected from the immediate relatives of living patients, medical records and, especially helpful in cases where the patient was deceased, details of their last hospitalization and death certificates. The mean ages at admission and at follow-up among schizophrenics, were 29 and 64 respectively.

There was sufficient information on 186 patients for their outcome to be rated according to the specified criteria for marital, residential, occupational, and psychiatric status at follow-up. Sixty-seven per cent never married; 12 per cent were divorced or separated; and 21 per cent were either married or widowed. Eighteen per cent were still in psychiatric hospital; 48 per cent at nursing or convalescent homes; and 34 per cent were living either in their own home or at the home of a relative. Fifty-eight per cent were incapacitated by mental illness; 8 per cent were incapacitated by physical illness; and 35 per cent were either employed or retired. Fifty-four per cent had incapacitating mental symptoms; 26 per cent had some symptoms; and 20 per cent were completely free of any psychiatric symptoms.

What are we to make of these figures? In general, it was noted that the outcome for schizophrenic patients was less favourable in all four outcome categories than for surgical patients. Death-rates in particular, when compared with those of the general population of Iowa, were found to be higher in sufferers from schizophrenia and mood disorder, but not among surgical patients. These high death-rates were mainly due to suicides and accidental deaths. In patients with mood disorder, these occurred mainly during the first decade of the follow-up, but among schizophrenic patients, they were spread evenly throughout the 40-year period.

Although the Iowa study, unlike the Swiss study, selected only schizophrenics who had been ill for at least six months, the percentages of schizophrenic subjects with no psychiatric symptoms at follow-up were very similar, ranging from 20 to 27 per cent. The percentages of schizophrenic patients living outside institutions were also similar, ranging from 34 to 43 per cent. However, owing to differences in the definition of schizophrenia in the two studies, it is harder to make comparisons with regard to general outcome, other than to note that patients selected for study in Iowa seemed to have a poorer outcome than those in Switzerland.

Other studies in the United States, such as that conducted by Dr Courteney Harding, now at the University of Colorado, have reported far higher rates of remission, with up to 68 per cent of patients found to be free of symptoms at a 32-year follow-up. Discrepancies of this magnitude are difficult to account for and pose a considerable and continuing challenge for clinicians attempting to forecast outcome.

Factors affecting outcome

As the research projects described above have shown, differences in outcome studies may be due to factors as fundamental as the definition of schizophrenia adopted or the geographic area in which the study is conducted.

A far higher degree of unanimity exists with regard to factors likely to affect outcome among schizophrenics. We know a great deal more about this as the information in question comes from an extremely wide range of sources: case studies, medical records, clinical observation, anecdotal evidence, and formal statistical analyses have all served to furnish us with a list of factors which are almost universally accepted. This information is well suited to presentation as a simple table:

Factors affecting prognosis in schizophrenia

Positive prognosis	**Negative prognosis**
Late onset	Early onset
Sudden onset	Gradual onset
Shorter duration of illness	Longer duration of illness
Normal affect (emotional response)	Affective (emotional) blunting
Awareness of mental problems	No awareness of mental problems
Obvious precipitating factors	Absence of precipitating factors
High socioeconomic status	Low socioeconomic status
Higher IQ	Lower IQ
Normally developed brain ventricles	Enlarged brain ventricles
Presence of manic or depressive symptoms	Absence of manic or depressive symptoms
Episodes of confusion	No episodes of confusion
Good social adjustment prior to onset	Poor social adjustment prior to onset
Presence of manic depression among relatives	Absence of manic depression among relations
Female gender	Male gender
Support of family	Lack of contact with family
Support of friends, workmates	Unemployment and social isolation
Married	Unmarried

Prognostic features of other cultures

The factors identified above are, in common with the great majority of research data into schizophrenia that we possess, the result of studies conducted in developed Western countries. We have already discussed the difficulties of comparing outcome studies, and it is reasonable to assume that comparisons across cultural boundaries are likely to be more unreliable still. Nonetheless, having touched on the issue of culture while discussing the possibility that many of our own mental health problems are due in part to the stressful nature of Western life, it is worth briefly examining outcome studies from other cultures.

In Africa, the outcome criteria set out above were found to be more applicable to those who led 'Westernized lives', especially those able to read and write. There may, of course, be a degree of self-selection at work here, since non-Westernized Africans would attribute their condition to traditional causes such as spirit possession or curses made by enemies.

A study of psychoses in Indonesia identified a state termed 'acute confusional state' which was markedly similar to schizophrenia. It was, however, reported as being due to various external causes, such as infection or vitamin deficiency, and showed a generally good outcome. However, chronic forms of schizophrenia were also found, with manifestations similar to those observed in Europe.

A study conducted on the island of Mauritius appeared to show far more favourable outcomes for schizophrenic people than those that occur in the West.

Although, as commonly occurs, the diagnostic criteria employed did not match those used in standard Western studies, the researchers believed that the key determinant of outcome was not differences in methodology but rather genuine cultural factors. In Mauritius, a higher percentage of patients examined at follow-up functioned normally, and were without symptoms. They had fewer relapses between time of discharge and follow-up; contrary to findings in Western cultures, symptoms of social withdrawal were not necessarily associated with poor outcome; nor manifestations of excitement related to good outcome.

Cultural factors within a given country will almost certainly change with time. This was vividly demonstrated by a study conducted in Japan, comparing schizophrenic patients admitted to hospital during four different periods from 1939 to 1963. To express the results very generally, it was found that symptoms of excitement had become progressively rarer during this time, while social withdrawal had become more common. The investigators speculated that changes in cultural values, knowledge about mental health as well as the development of a social welfare system and changes in treatment procedures had contributed significantly to these changes.

To date, one of the most helpful cross-cultural studies we possess is the *International Pilot Study of Schizophrenia (IPPS)*, conducted by the **World Health Organization** and mentioned at the beginning of this book. This nine-country study involved nations as culturally diverse as Nigeria and Czechoslovakia and, within broad limits, was methodologically 'clean'. The outcome studies showed that patients from developing countries appear to enjoy far higher rates of remission and recovery. The percentage of patients falling into the 'good outcome' category was as high as 57 per cent in Nigeria and 48 per cent in India. In Denmark it was just 6 per cent. The figures relating to 'poor outcome' again saw the developed world faring poorly, with the United Kingdom (31 per cent) and Denmark (31 per cent) doing worst. Nigeria (5 per cent) and the former Soviet Union (11 per cent) exhibited the lowest rates.

The general trend of these findings was supported when the WHO sponsored another ten-country study of schizophrenia during the same decade. Once again, the developing countries exhibited differences in recovery rates too great to be dismissed as the result of diagnostic discrepancy or lack of methodological rigour. To what can we attribute these results?

The answer, strange as it may seem, is that developing countries are *practising* concepts of care to which the developed world is at present merely paying lip service: in brief, they are *caring for their mentally ill in the community*. Researchers for the WHO study reported that the most important cultural factors implicated in the improved outcome for patients in developing countries were: close family ties, extended families, active participation of the family in the care of patients still receiving hospital treatment, and other factors which make it easier for patients to return to their previous lives.

Highly developed countries, in contrast, are characterized by the very factors that can make readjustment to normal life difficult. To mention but a few: family units are usually small and often dispersed; modern working techniques foster little sense of social cohesion; years of state welfare provision have engendered an attitude of reliance on others to solve personal problems; high levels of unemployment result in economic stress among those used to having high standards of living and so on—the list is depressingly long.

If a highly industrialized society inhibits the recovery and rehabilitation of schizophrenic patients, perhaps certain elements of agricultural society ought to be imitated to facilitate the treatment and recovery of schizophrenics in every type of society. The idea is not without its logic, but our personal opinion is that such a scheme is unlikely to work. From a clinical point of view, each patient is unique and will exhibit a unique outcome. Treatment should, therefore, be tailored according to each person's needs and the outcome judged accordingly. The wholesale importation of artificial and culture-specific treatment methods is unlikely to prove beneficial.

This is not to say that we have little or nothing to learn from developing cultures, but rather that the lessons may be social rather than clinical. The help that the community at large, and families in particular, can offer the schizophrenic need not be culture-specific; patience, consideration, and tolerance are abundant in every country, our own included. If they were not, we might as well join Thomas Szasz in his vision of the 'sick society'.

18

Summary

A challenge for us all

Statistically, wherever in the world you happen to live, the chances are roughly one in a hundred that you will at some time in your life suffer from schizophrenia. While you may well recover from an initial bout and never be troubled again by the condition, you may need to take powerful drugs to minimize the chance of relapse. In about one in ten cases, you will require almost constant care for the rest of your life. A roughly similar proportion will commit suicide.

The psychiatric and scientific community frankly admits that it knows comparatively little about the cause of the illness, its relationship with other conditions, and its responsiveness to treatment. As regards a cure, there are many theories on the subject, but no-one seriously proposes that one is within sight.

The system of care for schizophrenic people is in a state of upheaval and the community at large openly frightened of an illness it knows little about, save what it has acquired from often lurid media reporting.

It is to the 'average, normal' member of society that our final words are addressed: the key to some, if not all, of the problems enumerated above lies within his or her hand.

More and better research into the illness is urgently needed; the mental health-care system is crying out for funds commensurate with its aims and responsibilities; an enlightened public understanding of schizophrenia and other mental illnesses demands educational and promotional resources to counter the negative images of the illness encountered in society at large.

None of this can be achieved without money. Whether paid to the state as taxes or donated to charities or foundations, it is only through the willingness of the ordinary person to *pay* for improved mental health services and research that these changes can come about.

'Why', it may be asked, 'should ordinary people care?' If they are not among the unfortunate one in a hundred sufferers and are kept separate and safe from them, is this not enough? If we are not to renege on our promise to the mentally ill, the answer must be 'no'; for *care*, vague and unquantifiable as it is, is exactly what they have been assured they will receive.

Only a concerted programme of public education and awareness, coupled with a massive increase of resources for clinical research and practical care will suffice to guarantee the schizophrenic individual his or her 'care in the community'.

The success or failure of this policy is a litmus test of the true civilization and moral worth of our society. We are best judged not by the success with which we suppress or conceal from view our less conventional members, but by how well we assimilate and protect them, through learning, work and ultimately, love.

Appendix:

List of family and patient support groups

United Kingdom
MIND (National Association
for Mental Health)
Granta House
London E15 4BQ
Tel: 0181 519 2122

Mental Health Foundation
37 Mortimer Street
London W1N 8JU
Tel: 0171 580 0145

National Schizophrenia
Fellowship / VOICES
28 Castle Street
Kingston-upon-Thames
Surrey KT1 1SS
Tel: 0181 547 3937
Southern Region: 01256 841087
Midland Region: 01926 641048

Making Space
46 Allen Street
Warrington WA2 7JB
Tel: 01925 571 680

SANE
199–205 Old Marylebone Road
London NW1 5QP
Tel: 0171 724 6520

SANELINE – 0345 67 8000
(Telephone helpline open 2pm –
midnight every day of the year to
give information and support).

Schizophrenia Association
of Ireland
4 Fitzwilliam Place
Dublin 2
Republic of Ireland
Tel: 003531 6761 988

USA
National Alliance for the
Mentally Ill
200 North Glebe Road
Suite 1015
Arlington
Virginia 22203–3754
Tel: (001) 703 524 7600
Fax: (001) 703 524 9094

National Mental Health
Association
1021 Prince Street
Alexandria
Virginia 22314–2971
Tel: (001) 703 684 7722
Fax: (001) 703 684 5968

The National Alliance for
Research on Schizophrenia and
Depression
60 Cutter Mill Road
Suite 404
Great Neck
New York 11021
Tel: (001) 516 829 0091
Fax: (001) 516 487 6930

Australia
Schizophrenia Australia
Mail 223
McKean Street
North Fitzroy
Victoria 3068
Tel: (006) 03 9482 4387
Fax: (006) 03 9482 4871

Canada
Schizophrenia Society of Canada
814–75 The Donway West
Don Mills
Ontario M3C 2E9
Tel: (001) 416 4458204
Fax: (001) 416 4452270

Further reading

Andreasen, N.C. (1984). *The broken brain: The biological revolution in psychiatry*. Harper & Row, New York & London.

Bogerts, B. (1993). Recent advances in the neuropathology of schizophrenia. *Schizophrenia Bulletin*, **19**, 431–45.

Fuller, T.E. (1988). *Surviving schizophrenia: A family manual*, (revised edn). Harper & Row, New York & London/Fitzhenry & Whiteside, Markham, Ontario.

Gottesman, I.I. (1991). *Schizophrenia genesis: The origin of madness*. Freeman, New York.

Jablensky, A. (1995). Schizophrenia: Recent epidemiologic issues. *Epidemiologic Reviews*, **17**, 10–20.

Jeffries, J.J., Plummer, E., Seeman, M.V., and Thornton, J.F. (1990). *Living and working with schizophrenia*, (2nd edn). University of Toronto Press, Ontario.

McNeil, T.F. (1995). Perinatal risk factors and schizophrenia: Selective review and methodological demands. *Epidemiologic Reviews*, **17**, 107–12.

Meltzer, H.Y., Lee, M.A., and Ranjan, R. (1994). Recent advances in the pharmacotherapy of schizophrenia. *Acta Psychiatrica Scandinavica*, **90**(suppl. 384), 95–101.

Seidman, L.J., Cassens, G.P., Kremen, W.S., and Pepple, J.R. (1992). Neuropsychology of schizophrenia. In *Clinical syndromes in adult neuropsychology: The practitioner's handbook*, (ed. R.F. White), pp. 381–449. Elsevier, Amsterdam.

Tsuang, M.T. and Faraone, S.V. (1994a). Epidemiology and behavioral genetics of schizophrenia. In *Biology of schizophrenia and affective disease*, (ed. S.J. Watson), pp. 163–95. Raven, New York.

Tsuang, M.T. and Faraone, S.V. (1994b). Schizophrenia. In *Medical basis of psychiatry*, (ed. G. Winokur and P. Clayton), (2nd edn), pp. 87–114. W.B. Saunders, Philadephia.

Walsh, M. (1985). *Schizophrenia: Straight talk for family and friends*. William Morrow, New York / Warner Books, New York (paperback).

Weinberger, D.R. (1994). Schizophrenia as a neurodevelopmental disorder: A review of the concept. In *Schizophrenia*, (ed. S.R. Hirsch and D.R. Weinberger), pp. 293–323. Blackwood, London.

Index

Page numbers in bold indicate main entry

Index

Index